Praise for *The Success Principles*

D0871048

If you could only read one book this year, you have ⸱
—Harvey Mackay, author of the #1 *New York Times* bestseller
Swim with the Sharks Without Being Eaten Alive

In this one book, *The Success Principles Workbook* will guide you through the implementation of the basic strategies for creating success in any area of your life plus the advanced strategies to help you become a master of success.
—John Gray, Ph.D., author of *Men Are from Mars, Women Are from Venus*

In this powerful companion to the bestselling classic *The Success Principles*, Jack Canfield will walk you step-by-step through the implementation of the most powerful strategies for success. Whether you are just starting out or just wanting to take your already successful life to the next level, this practical guide will help get you there.
—John Assaraf, *New York Times* bestselling author of
Having It All and *The Answer*, MyNeuroGym.com

Jack Canfield's work has had a massive impact on my own success in life. Now he is sharing the core of his work in this practical, easy-to-implement *Workbook*. I strongly encourage you to follow this clear roadmap for creating whatever you want in both your personal and professional life.
—Marci Shimoff, #1 *New York Times* bestselling author of
Chicken Soup for the Woman's Soul and *Happy for No Reason*

A guru is one who brings you from the darkness into the light. Jack Canfield is a success guru. In *The Success Principles Workbook*, he gently guides you from the darkness of chaos and confusion, lack, and limitation into the light of realizing that you can do what may once have seemed impossible to do. If you are ready to "*do the work*" required to usher yourself and your life to the next level, get ready to shine because *The Success Principles Workbook* is the on switch you have been praying for.
—Iyanla Vanzant, author and host of *Iyanla: Fix My Life* (OWN)

Jack Canfield is a true master. He understands what it takes to lead a successful life, and in *The Success Principles Workbook* he puts all the key elements together in one place for the rest of the world to learn and use.
—T. Harv Eker, #1 *New York Times* bestselling
author of *Secrets of the Millionaire Mind*™

My good friend Jack Canfield is one of the most insightful speakers and teachers in the world today. After you have spent time working through this *Workbook* with him, internalizing his ideas and insights, you will be changed in a positive way for the rest of your life.
—Brian Tracy, one of America's leading authorities on the development of human potential and personal effectiveness and author of *Success Is a Journey, Million Dollar Habits,* and *The Traits of Champions*

Everything, and I mean everything, Jack Canfield does is a 10 on a scale of 10! Seriously, don't spend a moment delaying your success. Jack's *The Success Principles Workbook* is sure to help you effortlessly monetize your passions!!!
—Janet Bray Attwood, *New York Times* bestselling author of *The Passion Test*

In business and in life, there are just some people who've mastered the art of making better decisions, setting better goals, and doing a better job of focusing on the daily tasks that deliver desired outcomes. Jack Canfield is that person in spades. Luckily, he's put his formula into *The Success Principles Workbook* for the rest of us. Expect more out of life, your career, and your future when you read this book.
—Mark Thompson, *New York Times* bestselling coauthor of *Success Built to Last* and the world's #1 leadership coach for fast-growth companies

I have known and respected Jack Canfield for over 30 years. Jack is known in the world as a Master Teacher of Success. He has decades of experience in leading others to greater and greater heights of the success they dream of. He has codified the Laws of Success and now, in his new work, he and his coauthors guide you in exactly how to bring about the success you want. This book will change your life.
—Mary Morrissey, inspirational speaker, executive consultant, and founder of Brave Thinking Institute

Over the last 30 years, millions of Guthy-Renker customers have used our products to look better, feel better, and create a better life. But the most successful people I've seen—both customers and our brand and celebrity partners—do three things: they decide what they want, they create a plan, and they take action. Now, instead of going it alone, *The Success Principles Workbook* gives you the step-by-step process for getting to where you want to be. It's a very helpful tool and a great read.
—Bill Guthy, cofounder of Guthy-Renker

If you are looking for a magic bullet to improve your life, your career, and your relationships, *The Success Principles Workbook* delivers it in spades. But don't just buy this impressive new classic and put it on your shelf. Read the proven strategies, complete all the exercises and worksheets, and then get ready to join the ranks of the world's highest achievers!
—Raymond Aaron, Canada's #1 business and investment coach

The Success Principles Workbook is so simple to follow, but at the same time so powerful. This *Workbook* is as essential to achieving your goals as *The Success Principles* book itself. Jack has a way of making learning entertaining and fun. This workbook is a true lifesaver!
—Kathy Coover, cofounder and executive vice president of Isagenix International

The Success Principles Workbook is an amazing tool to help you get from where you are to where you want to be. Whether you are looking to increase your confidence, build your business, discover your passion and purpose, or simply get clear on your dreams and goals, Jack's timeless principles have been used by many of the world's most successful men and women both personally and professionally. As the founder of BNI, I have hired many of the world's best teachers to share their messages with my hundreds of thousands of members and I find him to be one of the best in the world.

—Ivan Misner, founder of BNI (Business Network International)
and *New York Times* bestselling author of *Networking Like a Pro*

If you truly want to know how to be more successful, Jack Canfield can teach you how. *The Success Principles Workbook* is a great resource for anyone who wants to become a master of their life!

—Natalie Ledwell, cofounder of Mind Movies and
bestselling author of *Never in Your Wildest Dreams*

No matter where you are with your life, *The Success Principles Workbook* helps you to implement proven strategies and time-tested systems to create a brighter future for yourself. Join the ranks of today's highest achievers in integrating and applying what this impressive new success tool offers you.

—Paul R. Scheele, Ph.D., author of *Natural Brilliance, Genius Code,
Abundance for Life,* and *The PhotoReading Whole Mind System*

There are people that you can watch have tremendous success. Then there are those rare teachers that give you the skill set for your individual success. Jack Canfield is the master at propelling you to your destiny. You should apply this book to your life today. I did and I have 5 *New York Times* bestselling books to show for it. What are you waiting for?

—Haylie Pomroy, #1 *New York Times* bestselling author of *The Fast Metabolism Diet*

You've been designed for greatness and a purpose. But how do you transform that sense of destiny into a workable plan that will bring you the ultimate life you want? Jack Canfield's *The Success Principles Workbook* is the tool you need. By helping you define your unique path to greatness, then encouraging you to take small steps every day, Jack Canfield helps you create the life you want. We loved it.

—Dr. Dave Braun and Dr. Troy Amdahl, internationally bestselling
authors of *Oola: Find Balance in an Unbalanced World*

Successful people know the most significant investment you can make is in yourself. *The Success Principles Workbook* helps you master the skill sets that will attract great people, great opportunities, and great fortune into your life. Let this investment pay off for you.

—Cynthia Kersey, CEO and founder, Unstoppable Foundation

Who doesn't want a healthy, vibrant, and compelling life? In *The Success Principles Workbook,* Jack Canfield defines the critical steps to creating the lifestyle, career, health, and well-being you want—plus his exercises, journaling prompts, and planning tools will help you set goals and take action to get there. If this is your year to make major changes, this book is the first one you need to read.

—Dr. Mark Hyman, 12-time *New York Times* bestselling author and founder of the UltraWellness Center

Success in any endeavor starts with a bias for action. Jack Canfield's well-written guide will inspire you to do those things that will bring about the career advancement, personal growth, standard of living, and financial wealth you desire. Whether you aspire to corporate leadership or want to chart your own course as an entrepreneur, *The Success Principles Workbook* will help you achieve the success you want.

—Dr. Halee Fischer-Wright, president and CEO of Medical Group Management Association and *New York Times* bestselling coauthor of *Tribal Leadership*

Implementation is everything! Think of *The Success Principles Workbook* as your personal coach and trainer on the road to success—guiding you to keep taking that next critical step that will lead you to the career and life you love and deserve.

—JJ Virgin, C.N.S., *New York Times* bestselling author of *The Virgin Diet*

The Success Principles is such an incredibly inspiring book. It's one of my all-time favorites! The storytelling is so mesmerizing that sometimes I lose track of the instruction that Jack Canfield has included within each story! I couldn't be more excited that Jack has released a companion workbook. It will allow us all to break down the lessons in the book in a way that we can implement today, so we can start achieving the success that Jack has dreamed of for us.

—Nick Nanton, Esq., Emmy® Award–winning director and producer of film and Broadway plays, *Wall Street Journal* bestselling author, and Global Shield Humanitarian Award recipient

If you want to impact millions and make millions in the process, then you need to take the right actions. *The Success Principles Workbook* gives you the step-by-step plan for becoming who you have always known you could be.

—Steve Harrison, cofounder of the National Publicity Summit and BestsellerBlueprint.com

THE
Success
Principles™
WORKBOOK

THE
Success
Principles™
WORKBOOK

AN ACTION PLAN FOR GETTING FROM WHERE
YOU ARE TO WHERE YOU WANT TO BE

Jack Canfield

with Dr. Brandon Hall
and Janet Switzer

WILLIAM MORROW
An Imprint of HarperCollins*Publishers*

THE SUCCESS PRINCIPLES WORKBOOK. Copyright © 2020 by Jack Canfield. All rights reserved. Printed in the United States of America. No part of this book may be used or reproduced in any manner whatsoever without written permission except in the case of brief quotations embodied in critical articles and reviews. For information, address HarperCollins Publishers, 195 Broadway, New York, NY 10007.

HarperCollins books may be purchased for educational, business, or sales promotional use. For information, please email the Special Markets Department at SPsales@harpercollins.com.

FIRST EDITION

Image on page 78 © digitalreflections/Shutterstock, Inc.
Image on page 42 © sibgat/Shutterstock, Inc.
Image on page 45 © Sensvector/Shutterstock, Inc.
Image on page 48 © MSSA/Shutterstock, Inc.
Image on page 50 © Yurchenko Yulia/Shutterstock, Inc.
Image on page 52 © studiostoks/Shutterstock, Inc.
Image on page 54 © Purple Clouds/Shutterstock, Inc.
Image on page 56 © HARAHI/Shutterstock, Inc.
Image on page 58 © Sensvector/Shutterstock, Inc.

Library of Congress Cataloging-in-Publication Data has been applied for.

ISBN 978-0-06-291289-3

20 21 22 23 24   LSC   10 9 8 7 6 5 4 3

CONTENTS

INTRODUCTION:
BEST PRACTICES FOR USING
YOUR WORKBOOK

*The most difficult part of any endeavor is
taking the first step, making the first decision.*

ROBYN DAVIDSON
Award-Winning Australian Author

What does it take to become a success at anything you want in life? What do the world's top achievers do to excel in their careers, finances, philanthropic endeavors, relationships, and more? Is there something special about them—qualities that other people simply don't have? Or is there a "secret formula" that we can all follow to help us succeed?

There is.

And for the past 40 years, I've made it my life's work to research, understand—then teach—these "secret" principles of success.

Of course, like most people, I was not brought up with any kind of self-help or human-potential concepts. I grew up in Wheeling, West Virginia; my mother was an alcoholic and my father was a workaholic. As a kid, I took summer jobs to make ends meet. And later, while I was fortunate enough to go to college on a scholarship, I paid for my books, clothes, and dates by serving breakfast in the campus dining hall. The money I earned never went very far. In fact, by the end of the month, I was so broke, you'd find me eating my famous "21¢ dinners"—a 10¢ can of tomato paste and garlic salt over an 11¢ bag of spaghetti noodles.

All that, however, was about to change.

After graduation, I was teaching high school history in inner-city Chicago when a chance job offer from insurance multimillionaire and personal-growth pioneer W. Clement Stone fostered a brand-new career for me: working for his foundation and teaching others the fundamental principles of success he had identified and written about in his bestselling books.

I immersed myself in this fascinating work. Not only did I vow to make it my own lifelong pursuit to study what works, I applied these principles to my own life, eventually started my own training company, and started teaching others these principles, too. It's a career path I've followed for more than 40 years.

Along the way, I discovered there's a series of principles by which successful people live. They don't always start with lots of money or high-level connections or other privileged circumstances, but they do take action on goals that matter. They plan and they focus and they persevere. They become constant learners. They keep score on the critical drivers of their success. They believe in themselves. They have a positive money consciousness. And they surround themselves with successful people.

These are the fundamentals by which I've lived my life, and they were the principles I was enthusiastically teaching in the late 1980s when repeated requests from audience members inspired me to collect the stories I told from stage into a book called *Chicken Soup for the Soul*®. When 144 publishers turned me down for the book, I again applied these principles and persevered until one publisher finally said yes.

Today, 26 years later—with 230 *Chicken Soup* titles in the series and more than 550 million books in print—these ground rules are still serving me in my career, relationships, pursuits, and life. My second book series, *The Success Principles*™, is the compendium of these proven fundamentals of success. It's now in 36 languages and has readers in 112 countries.★

But what about you? What can you do to achieve all that you want . . . and more?

As a follow-up, companion guide to *The Success Principles*, this workbook is designed to help you get from where *you* are to where you *want* to be. Whether you've read the original *Success Principles* book or not, you're in the right place. This *Workbook* is designed with both readers in mind.

If you're already familiar with the success principles, this *Workbook* will help you put them into daily practice. And if you're new to personal-growth work, each chapter will give you the essential information you need to learn, understand, and put into action the individual principles you discover.

★You'll find *The Success Principles: How to Get from Where You Are to Where You Want to Be* at all major bookstores and online retailers in most major languages. Special editions for teens, life coaches, and other readers are available, too.

ALL THAT YOU WANT TO BE, DO, AND HAVE IS POSSIBLE BY COMPLETING THE CHAPTERS IN THIS BOOK

Throughout this book are 17 chapters detailing the most important principles I teach. These are the basics that will help you take control of your outcomes—and take the right actions toward achieving the life of your dreams.

We'll start with *Chapter 1*, the fundamental principle you must follow: *Take 100% Responsibility for Your Life.*

One of the most pervasive myths today is that we're *entitled* to a great life—that somehow, somewhere, someone (certainly not us) is responsible for filling our lives with continual happiness, exciting career options, nurturing family time, and blissful personal relationships simply because we exist. But the real truth—and the one lesson this entire workbook is based on—is that there's only *one person* responsible for the quality of the life you live.

That person is *you*.

When you realize that *you*—not your circumstances, not other people—are responsible for your success (or lack of it), your life will dramatically shift. When you accept that your actions (or your failure to act), your thoughts, your beliefs, the words you say to yourself, and the pictures you hold in your mind have tremendous sway over your results, then you will have taken the most important step of all toward a life of freedom, abundance and fulfillment. *Chapter 1* will teach you that you always have a choice about what you think and how you act. You have a choice in how you respond to life's events. Once you realize that, you'll have regained your power—the power to create the life you truly want.

Other chapters will follow to help you decide what you want, set and achieve goals, ask for what you want, clean up your incompletes, build a support network of smart people . . . and much more.

And within each chapter, you'll find a number of tools to help you apply what you learn. I'll even help you create a new habit around each principle, so you can sustainably implement it day after day. It's these kind of combined actions that will steadily bring you success.

So, what can you look forward to as you shortly turn the page and start your journey?

"Discovering More About You" Exercises & Worksheets

Within each chapter, exercises of different kinds will help you get into action applying *The Success Principles* to your life. The first of these is called *Discovering More About You*. For example, in *Chapter 14*, you'll learn to surround yourself with successful people. Author Jim Rohn once said, *"You are the average of the five adults you spend the most time with."*

Not only is that a powerful condemnation of the toxic and limiting people in your life, it's also a compelling wake-up call to surround yourself with *solution-oriented, possibility thinkers*. That's what top achievers do. They cultivate relationships with a core group of people who can help them on their path to success.

To help you apply this principle to your life, I provide an exercise and worksheet called *Your Current and Future Groups* that asks you to list the people you spend time with—then evaluate whether they're *a benefit or an obstacle* to your growth, progress, and success. The worksheet called *Your Ideal Mentors* asks you to create a list of at least 10 people with specific skills—either by name or description of their job title—from whom you could learn the most. I often ask my national sales audiences how many attendees know the name of the top salesperson in their company. After virtually everyone raises their hand, I ask, *"How many of you have approached that person to ask their strategies for success? And how many of you have asked that person to mentor you?"* Virtually no one raises their hand. This exercise will help you surround yourself with successful people.

And other, similar exercises and worksheets are included in every chapter.

Make-It-a-Habit Worksheets

Did you know it takes 21 to 30 days of repeated action to create a new habit in your life? Habits are those things we do almost without thinking, and—for better or worse—these habits put our life on autopilot toward success or mediocrity. To help you put your own success on autopilot, I've featured *Make-It-a-Habit* worksheets in each chapter that are designed to help you sustainably practice that principle, every day or every week, for the rest of your life.

What's an example of these worksheets? In *Chapter 7: Take Action!*, I reveal that taking action toward your goals not only skyrockets your confidence, it puts you in the game doing what you need to do instead of keeping you on the sidelines—a spectator who's only thinking about or talking about what you want. To help you create the daily habit of being in action toward your goals, I feature a worksheet called Practice the Rule of 5—where, every morning, you can record those five tasks you must achieve by the end of the day.

Your Life Success Journal

Of course, once you've completed the exercises, it's time to permanently embed these lessons and insights into your consciousness by frequently reviewing what you've learned. I've included an easy tool for that: at the back of this workbook is *Your Life Success Journal*—a section where you can record the insights you learned along the way. At the end of each chapter, you'll be prompted to find the appropriate pages in the *Life Success Journal*, answer a few questions, and make notes about your newfound knowledge. This way, once you've completed the *Workbook*, you'll be able to quickly locate what was most important to you.

Affirmations

Finally, each chapter contains an *affirmation* for you to use as you're assimilating that principle into your life.

Affirmations are vividly detailed statements of you living, working, and enjoying life *as if your goals had already been achieved*. Affirmations help the brain focus on bringing about your heartfelt desires. *I'm happily depositing my first $100,000 royalty check as a bestselling author*, is one example of an affirmation. *I'm joyfully receiving the company's top sales award*, is another.

How Do Affirmations Work?

As scientists now know, the brain is a goal-seeking organism. If you give it a compelling, colorful, crystal-clear image of what you want—by frequently repeating an affirmation statement that describes that "want"—it will work night and day to create the opportunities, contacts, resources, and circumstances needed to achieve that vision. In fact, the brain has a special part called the *reticular activating system* that filters through the millions of impressions, images, sensations, messages, and thoughts it processes each day and passes to your conscious mind that specific information which will help you reach your goal.

I'll talk more about the power of affirmations in *Chapter 5*. But before then, you'll notice an affirmation at the beginning of each chapter. As you're working on a single chapter, I recommend that you repeat its affirmation several times a day. As you read, feel the positive emotions that arise—joy, pride, confidence, gratitude—as you experience achieving that goal in your mind's eye.

OUR ROLES: MINE AND YOURS

As I share with you the principles and lessons I've researched and implemented over a lifetime, you'll discover that—while you and I are in this process together—*practicing what it takes to create success* is up to you. Whether it's having more money, experiencing more fulfilling relationships, enjoying more time off, making a greater difference in the world, or being the person you know you were meant to be, I can only provide you with a *practical plan* for implementing these principles and making their use a habit—today, tomorrow, and for the rest of your life.

That's my role.

Your Role

This is where you come in. It's one thing for me to share this knowledge with you. But it's something else entirely for you to *take action* on this newfound knowledge. This is not a book for you simply *to read*. Rather, it's a book for you *to do*. Your *doing* will make all the difference in getting the life you want.

HOW TO GET THE MOST FROM THIS BOOK

What's the best way to get the most from this workbook? Be willing to take these principles seriously—as though your future depended on it. Catch yourself if you start to think, *I already know about this* (especially if you've already read the original *The Success Principles* book). Instead, ask yourself, *But am I doing this?* And then think about how your application of an individual principle can benefit you and bring about the life you want.

Commit to Studying One Chapter a Week . . . Or More

Read one chapter a week and complete all of its exercises—a commitment that should take about one to two hours of your time. Then, during the next seven days, allow the ideas you just learned to simmer. Practice the *Make-It-a-Habit* daily activities from that chapter during the week, too.

Finally, When You're Ready, Make "The Decision"

At some point, as you're studying and applying these principles—or when you've tested enough of these principles for yourself—you might find yourself on the brink of a very important decision: whether or not, once and for all, you'll take a stand on behalf of your own future.

After all the books you've read and the self-improvement programs you've tried, you might realize that what's really needed now is your *commitment* to stick with this *Workbook* to the very end and practice these success principles in earnest—perhaps for the rest of your life.

Remember, *the principles always work, if you always work the principles.*

It might be difficult. It might be uncomfortable. It might require you to do things you never believed you could do before. But your newly focused and success-oriented life can only begin when you *make the decision* to stick with the process, follow the directions, take one step at a time, and complete the chapters in this *Workbook* week after week. Along the way, you may also decide that you'll fully adopt these principles and make them an ongoing part of your life—not just for the rest of your life, but for the *best* of your life.

Your Option: Find a Success Partner and Make This Journey Together

While there's great value in going through this *Workbook* on your own, you'll experience even more impact if you find a partner and go through the *Workbook* together. Just like having a yoga buddy or a running partner, you can encourage and support each other through the process, have fun together, and increase the likelihood of staying on track with your progress.

MY PROMISE TO YOU

Here's my pledge to you: By learning these principles and following their guidelines, your life will never be the same. You'll not only experience the freedom of knowing you're in charge of your own destiny, you'll have the knowledge and power you need to take the action required to create the success you long for.

Yes. It is possible.

You have what you need in your head . . . and in your hands. Be assured that hundreds of thousands have come before you—learning and applying these principles with great success. It *is* truly possible for you to experience profound, rapid, and lifelong change, too. These principles work. Learn them and apply them.

FINALLY, STAY IN TOUCH!

We'd love to stay connected with you on your journey. Engaging, asking questions, and celebrating your wins is proven to further your success even more, so make a commitment to stay connected!

We look forward to hearing about your breakthroughs and successes.

Please send us your thoughts at workbook@jackcanfield.com or tag us on social media!

- @jackcanfield_official
- @jackcanfieldfan
- @jackcanfield
- @canfieldjack

THE
Success
Principles™
WORKBOOK

PART ONE

The Fundamentals of Success

Success is neither magical nor mysterious.
Success is the natural consequence of consistently
applying the basic fundamentals.

JIM ROHN
Motivational Philosopher

TAKE 100% RESPONSIBILITY FOR YOUR LIFE

*The moment I take responsibility for everything in my life
is the moment I gain power to change anything in my life.*

Affirmation Based on a Quote by
HAL ELROD

In ancient days, architects and builders had few measuring tools. As a result, the most important step when building a structure was the placement of the very first block of stone. All the remaining stones were placed based on this first stone: *the cornerstone.*

The cornerstone of all the success principles is this one: Take 100% responsibility for your life. Everything else rests upon fully understanding and applying this principle. If you are really finally ready to begin to do what it takes to go achieve your next level of success, happiness, and the fulfillment you desire, then I want you to fully commit yourself to the study and application of this principle.★

If there were an easier way to have the life of your dreams, believe me, I would tell you. Really. I learned this first principle myself more than 30 years ago, and it has made all the difference in the success that I and the hundreds of thousands of my students have achieved.

★ Read *Principle 1: Take 100% Responsibility For Your Life* in the book *The Success Principles* for more explanation, stories, and examples.

TAKE RESPONSIBILITY

To take 100% responsibility for your life and your results means that you accept the fact that you are the one in charge of all the results you produce. When you fully realize that you—not your circumstances and not other people—are responsible for your success or lack of success, your life will dramatically shift. When you realize that it is your actions or lack of action, your thoughts and beliefs, and the pictures that you create in your mind, then you will have taken the most important step you can take toward a life of freedom, abundance, and fulfillment. When you realize you always have a choice in every moment about what you think and how you act, you will have reclaimed your power—the power to create the life you truly want.

There is an important formula that captures the simple essence of this truth.

$$E + R = O$$
$$EVENT + RESPONSE = OUTCOME$$

The essence of this formula is that everything you are currently experiencing (your current **O**utcomes) are the result of how you **R**esponded to earlier **E**vents in your life. And if you don't like your current outcomes (your health, your weight, your income, your total savings, the quality of your possessions, the quality of your relationships, your level of happiness, your golf score, your job, your sales numbers, where you live . . . everything you currently have and are experiencing), then you have to change the way you are responding to the events that show up in your life!

Let me give you an example.

Let's say you are given a $4,000 bonus at the end of the year. That's an event. One response, after taxes are taken out, is to invest the remaining $3,200. The outcome of that is that one year later you have an additional net worth of $3,394. If your response is to spend your bonus, you have no additional net worth. Same event . . . two different outcomes.

Here's another example. Someone offers you a large piece of chocolate cake at the office party. One response is to eat it. The outcome from that would be to put on more weight. The other response would be to politely refuse it, saying you are cutting back on your sugar intake, and the outcome from that is you maintain your body weight.

Life is 10 percent what happens to you and 90 percent how you respond to it.

LOU HOLTZ
Legendary College Football Coach and ESPN Analyst

There are only three responses (R's) that you have any control over—your thoughts, the visual images that you create in your mind, and your behavior, which includes what you say (or don't say) and your actions (what you do or what you don't do). That is all you have control over.

You might be asking, "What about feelings? Aren't they a response?" Actually 99% of feelings are an outcome of how you think about something. If you reject me, in order for me to feel sad or angry, I have to first think a thought like, *No matter what I do, nobody ever accepts and includes me; I am going to be alone forever.*

One of the greatest differences between successful people and those who would merely like to be is how they respond to the events and opportunities in their lives. Here is another example of the same event, with different responses producing different outcomes.

Event	+ Your Response	= Outcome
Your spouse forgets your birthday.	You tell yourself, "S/he forgot my birthday. That means s/he doesn't love me."	You feel sad and depressed, and your self-esteem takes a hit.

Event	+ Your Response	= Outcome
Your spouse forgets your birthday.	You tell yourself, "Somebody who loves me forgot my birthday. I wonder what's going on with them?"	You end up feeling concerned, but you still have high self-esteem.

WHAT GETS IN THE WAY OF TAKING RESPONSIBILITY?

If taking responsibility for one's life were easy, everyone would do it. So, what's up? It turns out that it's easier to complain about the way things are, to blame others and to make excuses, than to change one's behavior. Changing is uncomfortable. It takes disciplined effort and intentionally stepping outside of one's comfort zone. And most people would rather be comfortable than uncomfortable. Let's take a deeper look at blaming, complaining, and excuse making.

BLAMING: YOU HAVE TO GIVE IT UP

When most people don't achieve the level of success they want in their life, they tend to blame people and things outside themselves. They blame their boss, their coworkers, their parents, their spouse, their children, economic conditions, high prices, Wall Street, the government, the other political party, the media, the traffic, and the weather.

The bad news: To have the success you want, you have to give up blaming. The good news: As soon as you do, you will experience greater power and energy in your life, and you will attract other positive and powerful people to be around you.

Blaming Mind-set:	It is not my fault. It's because of what they did. They are responsible.
Success Mind-set:	When I look beyond blaming, I can see how I actually created or allowed this, and I can begin to search for and find ways to get the result I want.

Once you realize that you created it the way it is, you then have the power to uncreate and re-create it the way you want it.

All blame is a waste of time. No matter how much fault you find with another, and regardless of how much you blame him, it will not change you.

WAYNE DYER
Author of *Change Your Thoughts—Change Your Life*

Take another look at blaming with this example.

Blaming	
Event:	Your coworkers continually miss deadlines, causing you to work late to bring projects in on time.
Your Response:	You blame your coworkers and management, but say nothing.
Outcome:	You end up working late many nights, straining your marriage and family relationships, and jeopardizing your health.

No Blaming	
Event:	Your coworkers continually miss deadlines, causing you to work late to bring projects in on time.
Your Response:	You find ways to streamline the process, and then quietly present your plan to the team leader.
Outcome:	The manager creates an expanded role for you, giving you more oversight on projects, which leads to increased responsibility, and eventually an increase in salary . . . and you are home earlier to spend time with your family and get more sleep.

The truth is, when confronted with a negative event, successful people look beyond blaming and finger-pointing. Instead, they look for new ways to resolve it. They *say something* or *do something* rather than blame someone.

HOW TO GIVE UP BLAMING

Are you *willing* to give up all blaming? That is the first question you need to ask yourself. If your answer is no, put away this workbook until you are ready to make some changes to get the success you want. If your answer is yes, great. Here is how to do it. The first step is to recognize and acknowledge the blaming that you have been doing up until now.

DISCOVERING MORE ABOUT YOU:
Blaming

Check ☑ any of the following blaming thoughts that you have used to justify your current life situation.

I don't have the success I want because:

☐   I had a difficult childhood. It's my family's fault.

☐   The college I went to was not very good. It's their fault.

☐   My spouse doesn't support my dreams. It's his/her fault.

☐   The company I work for doesn't respect me or my ideas. The management is to blame for how I feel.

☐   My friends aren't very ambitious, so neither am I. It's their fault.

☐   The reason I am broke is because the economy is terrible/my company doesn't pay a fair wage/my spouse spends every penny I make/my kids are spoiled/immigrants have taken all the jobs/all the good jobs have moved offshore.

☐   I'm overweight because of the food my wife cooks.

Add your own:

1. Up until now, I have blamed _____

   for _____.

2. Up until now, I have blamed _____

   for _____.

3. Up until now, I have blamed _____

   for _____.

The statements you have written above may in fact be true, but they do not need to continue to stop you from going after the success you want. You can change those blaming thoughts to thoughts of responsibility.

For each of the statements you wrote above, write a new "no-blame" thought to replace it. Here are a couple of examples:

Blaming:	The reason I'm not more successful is because my spouse doesn't support my dreams.
No-Blaming Thought:	Even though my spouse may not support my dreams, I can still take the necessary actions to create a better life.
Blaming:	The reason I'm not making more money is because I don't have any real options.
No-Blaming Thought:	Even though I don't see any obvious options, the real reason I'm not making more money is because I haven't thought creatively and pursued new opportunities.

No-Blaming Exercise

For each of the blaming thoughts you listed above, write a new no-blame thought of how you can be successful regardless.

1. Instead of blaming _____ for _____,

   I could do this: _____

2. Instead of blaming _____ for _____,

   I could do this: _____

3. Instead of blaming _____ for _____,

   I could do this: _____

Stretch opportunity! If you want to take it further after filling in your answers, go back and change the words "I could do this" above to "I will do this." Go ahead; try it out.

COMPLAINING: YOU HAVE TO GIVE IT UP

Do any of the following statements sound familiar?

> *My supervisor ignored the special report she requested—again!*
> *My spouse constantly hounds me about the way I eat.*
> *The yoga instructor always starts late.*

Here is what's interesting about complaining: In order to complain, you have to know there is something better available that you would prefer . . . but that you are not willing to take the necessary action to create. You would rather complain because it protects you from having to take the risk to create it the way you want. When you complain, what you're really saying is, *"I have something I prefer, but I'm not willing to risk creating it . . . so I'll complain to you instead."*

If you complain about your spouse hounding you about the way you eat, you have to have in mind what you would prefer: either for your current spouse to leave you alone, or for a different spouse who doesn't hound you—like the spouse you have seen at a friend's house or on a TV show.

Have you noticed that people don't complain about gravity? It's because they know they can't change it. People do complain about their jobs because they know there is a better job out there somewhere, but choose not to change jobs. People do complain about the weather, because they know there is someplace with better weather and that they could move there. But they choose not to, so they complain instead.

Complaining can dissipate some of the energy of an upset, but it doesn't change the outcome you are experiencing. It also keeps you feeling powerless. With each complaint you express, you give away more of your power. If you want to be successful, you have to stop complaining—now! You will need all of your mental, emotional, and physical strength to take the actions you need to take to go after the success you want.

I know it's common to complain. It is often socially acceptable, even expected and affirmed, in many groups. If complaining is the norm for the people you spend time with, if you find yourself in an "Ain't It Awful!" club, you need to quit that club. If they won't stop complaining, you have to stop spending time with them. You need to surround yourself with responsible, solution-oriented people.

DISCOVERING MORE ABOUT YOU:
Complaining

1. **Write down your four biggest complaints.**
   Consider work, family members, finances, body weight, traffic, or other.
   Sample Answers: It is so hard to lose these extra 10 pounds! My spouse keeps me up all night long with his/her snoring. The people on the town council are all corrupt.

   (a) _____

   (b) _____

   (c) _____

   (d) _____

2. **For each item you wrote above, write down what you *prefer* to have.** For the most benefit, start each line with, *I prefer to have . . .* and end each line with, *. . . but instead I complain about how . . .* (*Rewriting may seem tedious, but it allows for deeper learning.*)
   Sample Answer: I prefer to weigh 10 pounds less! But instead I complain about how hard it is to lose weight.

   (a) _____

   _____

(b)   _____

       _____

(c)   _____

       _____

(d)   _____

       _____

3. **Change your complaints to actions.**

   For each complaint in #1 above, complete this phrase: *Instead of complaining, I could do* _____
   to get what I want.

   Sample Answer: Instead of complaining, I could begin to exercise at least 30 minutes a day.

(a)   _____

       _____

(b)   _____

       _____

(c)   _____

       _____

(d)   _____

       _____

From now on, whenever you start to complain, you will more likely notice it and catch yourself. You may also be less likely to tolerate complaining from others as you realize there are actions they could take to resolve the situation if they chose to.

MAKING EXCUSES: YOU HAVE TO GIVE IT UP

Dear Reader: I was going to make this a better workbook for you, but I got tired. I ran out of ideas, and I didn't have enough time. Would you accept that? I hope not. Instead of offering excuses, I am offering you the best possible *Workbook*, based on research and best practices, for implementing the success principles. I am totally 100%

responsible for that. You are not interested in my excuses—only my results, so you'll get no excuses from me.

HOW EXCUSES STEAL YOUR FUTURE

When you don't achieve the result you want, or you don't have the life you want, it is natural and easy to make excuses. You hear people making excuses every day. Making excuses is a response to an event. It is a way of justifying your current results, but it is simply an ineffective response that does not produce a better result. Making excuses disempowers you and prevents you from thinking creatively about what you can do differently.

To create the life and success you desire, you will need to give up all your excuses. Let me say that again because it is so important: *To create the life and success you long for, you will need to give up all your excuses.* This includes all the reasons you give for why things are the way they are. When you take your focus away from your excuses, you will be able to see clearly why things are the way they are, and focus on what you can do to create what you want.

In the next exercise, you will have the chance to see in writing some of the excuses you're making that you may not recognize.

HOW TO RESOLVE A LONG-STANDING PROBLEM

In my workshops, I often pair people together and ask them to "coach" each other through the following exercise called the "Difficult or Troubling Situation Exercise," which helps resolve long-standing problems without blaming, complaining, or making excuses.

Difficult or Troubling Situation Exercise

Take a look at the sample responses below before completing the exercise for yourself on the next page.

1. What is a difficult or troubling situation in your life?

   I've been wanting to start my own training business for two years, but I keep putting it off.

2. How are you creating it or allowing it to happen?

   I keep putting off deciding exactly what I want to teach, and even deciding what to call the business.

3. What are you pretending not to know?

   It has been eating me up inside, and I want to get going.

4. What is the payoff for keeping it like it is?

   At least I won't make a mistake and look foolish to my friends and family.

5. What is the cost for not changing it?

   I'm miserable in my current job, and I'll remain miserable if I don't take action.

6. What would you rather be experiencing?

   I want to feel like I am walking my talk, that I am "all in" with my life, and that I'm fulfilling my true purpose by doing what I really long to do.

7. What actions will you take to create that?

   I will decide what topic to start with, create a new Web site, start blogging, and launch my new business.

8. By when will you take that action?

   By the end of next month. (Gulp! It's scary to commit to starting, but I know all the steps I need to take.)

9. On a scale of 1 to 10, how likely are you to follow through with that action?

   10! It has to be a 10. I have been waiting too long, and there is nothing stopping me except my own fear and hesitancy.

Many of the problems that remain unresolved for us are due to one thing: We don't see that we are part of the problem. We are not taking 100% responsibility for how we are creating it. The series of questions that follow will guide you through a powerful process to correctly define the problem, take ownership for how you are creating it, and clarify how to resolve it.

This exercise is best done with a partner, but it can also be done alone as a journal writing exercise just answering the questions on paper. If you can, find a friend or colleague you trust with whom to do this exercise. You will both benefit from it. Have your partner ask you each of the questions in order. After you complete answering the questions, switch roles and then ask your partner the questions.

Now it is your turn to answer the questions. If you have a partner, each of you will take a turn asking the other the entire list of questions. Don't respond to, suggest solutions, or judge each other's answers. Simply assist by asking the questions. If you are doing this exercise alone, simply ask yourself the questions and write down the answers.

Now It's Your Turn: Difficult or Troubling Situation Exercise

1. What is a difficult or troubling situation in your life?

_____

_____

_____

2. How are you creating it or allowing it to happen?

_____

_____

_____

3. What are you pretending not to know?

_____

_____

_____

4. What is the payoff for keeping it like it is?

_____

_____

_____

5. What is the cost for not changing it?

_____

_____

_____

6. What would you rather be experiencing?

_____

_____

_____

7. What actions will you take to create that?

_____

_____

_____

8. By when will you take that action?

_____

_____

_____

9. On a scale of 1 to 10, how likely are you to follow through with that action?

_____

_____

_____

How are you complicit in creating the conditions of your lives that you say you don't want?

JERRY COLONNA
Author of *Reboot: Leadership and the Art of Growing Up*

The principle of taking 100% responsibility for your life is not something you learn about once and it is solved for the rest of your life. It is more like staying fit. Every day you have to pay attention. Every day you can ask yourself, *Did I blame anyone today? Did I complain today, instead of taking action to change the situation? Did I make excuses today when I did not get the result I wanted or that I had promised?*

Taking 100% responsibility for everything in your life is a new way of thinking for most people. Over time, as you pay attention and live this principle, it will become second nature to you. Practicing and eventually mastering this fundamental principle is absolutely necessary in order to produce the results you want and to have the life you long for.

To take 100% responsibility for your life means you take ownership for all you do and for the results you produce. As you do that, your life will become less complicated and you will have the energy, power, and ideas to create the life you want. This is captured in the quote you may have heard before: "If it's meant to be, it's up to me."

ARE YOU CHANGING?

Growth = Awareness + Choice. You may not have noticed it fully yet, but reading this chapter and doing these exercises have likely begun to change you. You may begin to notice that something does not feel right when you or someone else starts to blame someone, complain about something, or make an excuse. Simply being aware of this is a huge step in itself. It provides the opening for you to choose a different and more effective response.

When you notice that you are complaining, blaming, or making excuses, you can pause and take a breath. Slow down, become present with yourself, and make a new choice. It is that simple. But it's not always easy! You have to stay vigilant. The more you stay aware and practice what you have learned, the easier and easier it will get over time until eventually it will become an unconscious habit.

Okay, you have now completed the *learning* portion of this chapter. However, since this is a *workbook*, designed for you to put these success principles to work in your life every day and to make their use a *habit*, there is still a little more *work* to do.

MAKE-IT-A-HABIT WORKSHEET
Take 100% Responsibility Today

I trust that you now see that to empower yourself to take action toward the success you want, you must be willing to give up blaming, complaining, and making excuses. In order to give up these behaviors, however, you must also become aware of when you are behaving this way.

To raise your awareness, conduct a *100% Responsibility Evening Review* every evening for a week. The purpose is to review your day and look for where you may have blamed, complained, or made excuses. Here's how to do that:

1. Complete the *100% Responsibility Evening Review* below, every evening for a week.
Every evening for the next seven days, reflect on your day and consider the following questions. Take your time and consider what you said to yourself, as well as what you may have said aloud to others. Many people find it easier to answer the questions when they close their eyes.

Note: Instead of giving you questions that can be answered by a simple yes or no, the questions that follow are designed to begin a "self inquiry" where you can review your day and identify those situations where you blamed, complained, or made excuses.

Blaming Review

Who did I blame today?
Example: *I attended a workshop today, and I blamed (in my thoughts) the person in charge, thinking he did not design the event very well.*

_____

_____

_____

_____

From the point of view of taking 100% responsibility, I see that . . .
Example: *Actually, I remember now that I did not bring a workbook as requested. I had to borrow a piece of paper, and that limited my ability to do the written work in a manner that would have allowed me to get more value from the activities.*

_____

_____

_____

_____

A more responsible statement, or an action to take next time, is:

Example: *Instead of blaming the person, even in my head, next time I will ensure I am fully prepared to participate.*

_____

_____

_____

_____

Complaining Review

What did I complain about today?

Example: *I was tired and sleepy a couple of times today and complained to others and myself about my low energy.*

_____

_____

_____

_____

From the point of view of taking 100% responsibility, I see that . . .

Example: *I have not been exercising much lately, and I've been eating more sugar than is good for me.*

_____

_____

_____

_____

A more responsible statement, or an action to take next time, is:

Example: *I will increase my exercise by 15 minutes a day for at least four days per week, beginning tomorrow.*

_____

_____

_____

_____

As you do this Evening Review and ask yourself these questions, remember to breathe! Relax. Be easy on yourself. You are not bad or wrong. It is a common habit to blame, complain, and make excuses. You are the exception for wanting to change that habit and to empower yourself to create a better life through taking 100% responsibility.

Making Excuses

What did I make an excuse about today?

Example: *Someone brought donuts to work today. Those crumb cake ones . . . my favorites. I wanted to ignore them, but I ate one. My excuse was that it was too hard for me to resist.*

_____

_____

_____

_____

From the point of view of taking 100% responsibility, I see that . . .

Example: *I was the one who chose to eat them. I may as well just drop the excuse. It doesn't add anything; it just makes me feel like a victim of my own lack of willpower. Instead, I affirm that how I respond to any event in life is up to me.*

_____

_____

_____

_____

A more responsible statement, or an action to take next time, is:

Example: *First, I can simply accept the fact that I <u>chose</u> to eat them. I can also use a tactic next time such as leaving the snack area right away whenever I see those crumb cake donuts!*

_____

_____

_____

_____

2. **Make a reminder for yourself—right now—to complete a *100% Responsibility Evening Review* each evening this week.**

If you are like most people, once you put down this workbook, you may forget about these ideas until you pick up the workbook again. In order to avoid this outcome, you will need to put in extra effort to implement your newfound behaviors. Here are several ways to make a reminder for yourself to do this evening review each night this week.

• Make a sticky note that says, *"100% Responsibility Evening Review"* and place it on the cover of this workbook. Place the workbook on your bedside table. You may also want to place a sticky note on your bathroom mirror.

• Set a timer on your smartphone for each evening this week with the label, "Evening Review."

• If you look at your daily calendar in the evening, write an appointment for yourself for your evening review.

3. Write a reminder card.
If you write in a journal regularly, write a reminder on a notecard and place the card in your journal where you will see it.

4. Take a picture.
Snap a picture of the questions with your smartphone for your personal use. Print it or store it where you will see it as a reminder.

Add to Your Life Success Journal

In the back of this Workbook is a section called *Your Life Success Journal* where you'll have the opportunity to record your key learnings from each chapter in an easy-to-locate place.

Go to the beginning of *Your Life Success Journal* now, on page 221.

CHAPTER

2

BE CLEAR WHY YOU'RE HERE: DETERMINE YOUR LIFE PURPOSE

I am passionately and joyfully pursuing my life's calling,
every day moving closer to achieving my goals.

AFFIRMATION

Determining our life purpose—and deciding how we are meant to express it in the world—is one of the most important actions that successful people take to create the lives they want. They take the time to understand what they're naturally good at and what they're meant to do—then they pursue that role with passion and enthusiasm. I believe that discovering your life purpose is one of the most important principles of success.

In this chapter, you'll not only discover what brings you joy and what you're passionate about, but you'll also determine the highest and best use of those skills and activities—for you . . . for your career . . . for your family . . . and for the world. You will gain valuable clarity on what your purpose is so you can start living a life of greater meaning, fulfillment, and success.★

BORN THIS WAY

After working with more than a million people all over the world, I have come to believe that each of us is born with a unique life purpose that's up to us to discover. Your purpose isn't something you need to make up; it's already there. You just have to uncover it. You are unique and your life purpose is unique, too.

★ Read *Principle 2: Be Clear Why You're Here* in the book *The Success Principles* for more explanation, stories, and examples.

You have a masterpiece inside you, you know. One unlike any that has ever been created, or ever will be. If you go to your grave without painting your masterpiece, it will not get painted. No one else can paint it. Only you.

GORDON MACKENZIE

A LIFE OF MEANING

Discovering your purpose is key to creating a life of meaning, fulfillment, and success. Clarifying and pursuing your life purpose will not only help you get the success you want, it will also make your journey more fulfilling and enjoyable. When your life purpose guides you, you can use your natural talents and abilities to accomplish what you want. When you're clear about your purpose, you will know which opportunities and choices are aligned with your purpose—and which are not.

MY OWN LIFE PURPOSE

I have made sure that the work I do is completely aligned with my purpose. That alignment is core to my success *and* to my satisfaction and joy in life. Here is my life purpose statement:

My life purpose is to inspire and empower people to live their highest vision in a context of love and joy, in harmony with the highest good of all concerned.

I live my purpose in several ways. I inspire people through the stories I tell, like in the 200+ *Chicken Soup* books that I compiled and edited, and in movies like *The Secret* and *The Soul of Success*. I empower others by teaching practical techniques in books like *The Success Principles* and through this *Workbook*, as well as through my live and online Breakthrough to Success and Train the Trainer programs. I have conducted trainings and seminars in more than 50 countries and have given more than a thousand speeches to over one million people. And I've enjoyed every minute of it because it's what I love to do, and it's in alignment with my life purpose.

WITHOUT A LIFE PURPOSE

For some people, though, it's a challenge to identify their life purpose. However, without a purpose in life, it's easy to get sidetracked on your life's journey, to wander and drift, accomplishing little. You may even have asked yourself at one point or another, *"What should I do with my life?"* Or you may enjoy what you do, but on deeper exploration, discover that you're passionate about something altogether different from what you currently are doing. Without a life purpose as the compass to guide you, even your greatest achievements may not fulfill you.

WHAT MAKES YOU COME ALIVE?

Where in your life do you find the most joy and fulfillment? The answers to these questions point directly to your life purpose.

> *Don't ask what the world needs. Ask yourself what makes you come alive, and go do that, because what the world needs is people who have come alive.*
>
> HOWARD THURMAN
> Author, Philosopher, Theologian, and Educator

Your purpose can provide you with inner guidance that tells you when you're on course or off course by the amount of joy you're experiencing. Those activities that bring you the greatest joy are the ones that are most in alignment with your life purpose. When you follow your joy, everything in life seems to fall into place. You're doing what you love to do, doing what you're good at, and accomplishing what's important to you. When you're on purpose, the people, resources, and opportunities you need seem to naturally gravitate toward you.

YOUR LIVELIHOOD

One of the keys to a happy life is to arrange things so that you spend more of your time doing things aligned with your purpose. When you're able to combine your livelihood with your life purpose, achieving the success and lifestyle you desire becomes much easier and more natural. With a clearly stated life purpose and a vision of what you want in your life,★ you can develop a clear set of criteria for making all your major life decisions (including your career) and for setting a lifetime's worth of meaningful and fulfilling goals.

A PURPOSE IS NOT A GOAL

It's important to be clear about the difference between a purpose and a goal. A *goal* is a specific target you want to reach by a certain time.† A life purpose is *not* about *having* something or *achieving* something. There is no end point to a purpose. Rather, it's about using your natural talents and *being* a certain way or *contributing* in a certain way. It's that which brings you joy and fulfillment whenever you do it.

Your *purpose* is your "Why." It's your ultimate reason for being. Then, with your purpose in mind, you can write your goals and achieve the results you want.

Your *goals*, on the other hand, are your "What." They state what you intend to do, accomplish, or have. When your goals are aligned with your purpose, they're meaningful for you, and you have more passion and perseverance to achieve them.

WHAT IF YOU'RE THINKING,
MY LIFE PURPOSE ISN'T RELATED TO MY WORK?

Stand by! Once you craft your purpose statement in the exercises that follow, we will address this issue.

★I will guide you through creating your life vision in *Chapter 3: Decide What You Want.*
†We will cover goals in *Chapter 4: Use the Power of Goal-Setting to Achieve Your Vision.*

YOUR PURPOSE IS YOUR PERSONAL NORTH STAR

For centuries, ships on the high seas relied on the night sky for navigation. In particular, they used the North Star, at the tail end of the Little Dipper. While all the other stars appeared to move across the sky with the Earth's rotation, only the North Star held its position. It served as a steadfast reference point with which sailors could determine the direction to follow.

Our life purpose serves as our own steadfast reference point, with which we can determine the direction we are to follow. This is especially relevant today, when we have so many options available to us. Our life purpose helps us decide among many possible paths, goals, and activities to pursue the ones most fulfilling and satisfying to us.

To determine your life's purpose—to develop it using crystal clear words that are compelling to you and others—take your time to complete the exercises that follow. Then, finish by writing your own heartfelt purpose statement.

The purpose of life is a life of purpose.

ROBERT BYRNE
American Chess Grandmaster

PURPOSE IS PERSONAL

Since your purpose is highly personal and meaningful to you, the *scope* of your purpose doesn't matter—not at all. A purpose statement usually includes some aspect of making a contribution, or doing something for others, in some way. When you're experiencing joy doing what you're doing, you are automatically contributing to others. Whatever that good is that you want to do, it's right for you and others will automatically benefit from it. Whether your purpose is to discover new medicines, or to raise your children with love and caring, your purpose is worthy and sufficient—and it's needed for the world to work. There is no satisfaction to be had in comparing the magnitude of your purpose with someone else's purpose. It's as personal as your favorite book or favorite song. While some people want to end hunger, others want to take cupcakes to the teachers at their neighborhood school. Whatever you're doing, as long as you're truly pursuing the expression of your unique purpose, it's as critical as ending hunger. If it gives you joy, then it's aligned with your purpose. Think about it. If everyone fulfilled their true purpose, all the needs in the world would be met. People who love to teach would teach. People who love to cook would feed everyone; people who love to fix things would be mechanics; people who love to write, paint, sing, dance, act, and play musical instruments would entertain us; and so on.

> Karen Gilmore-Hall says she realized her purpose during her teens. Now in her 30s, Karen says, "My purpose is to be kind and loving and helpful, and to enhance our mutual experience of life."
>
> She can be "on purpose" almost anywhere or at any time, she says, by encouraging others, helping others feel understood and cared for, and doing her best to be a good friend.
>
> "I try to put more love and smiles into the world," Karen says, "and believe that good begets good."

EXAMPLES OF LIFE PURPOSE STATEMENTS

Here are the life purpose statements of people from all backgrounds and interests, whether working locally or living out their purpose on a global stage.

My purpose is to use my talents in art and science to bring about the spiritual awakening of humankind.

SERGEY IVANENKO
Songwriter

My life purpose is to inspire every woman to realize her own personal beauty, regardless of her body type, size, or age, to love herself, and to live brilliantly.

RANI ST. PUCCHI
Fashion Designer and Author

My purpose is to use my skills as an educator to inspire, motivate, and empower others to find their light and to create the happiness they desire.

ROBYN ALLABY
Vice Principal

My purpose is to inspire young women everywhere to pursue their dreams with passion and an unrelenting drive for excellence.

KATRINA OKO-ODOI, PH.D.

*My purpose is to publish books of enduring beauty, integrity, and wisdom,
and to inspire others to fulfill their most cherished dreams.*

JANET MILLS
Coauthor with Don Miguel Ruiz of *The Four Agreements*

My purpose is to expand the world's compassion and connection.

JEFF WEINER
CEO of LinkedIn

DETERMINE YOUR LIFE PURPOSE STATEMENT

Now I'd like to help you uncover your life purpose statement.

The Structure of a Life Purpose Statement

After decades of helping others determine their life purpose, I have found a format that seems to work best for a clear and focused purpose statement. Work with these two guidelines and see if they work for you and your purpose statement:

• A single sentence
• Easily memorized

Why a Single Sentence?

When you hold your purpose statement to *a single sentence* it helps avoid the tendency to write long, all-inclusive statements. It helps to bring your purpose to a focus, and identify the essential elements. And it is easily learned and memorized.

Why Easily Memorized?

It's important to be able to *memorize* your purpose statement, so that you can call it to mind at any time, and easily share it with others. Your purpose statement isn't something you write down, file away, and then have to go and look up.

DISCOVERING MORE ABOUT YOU:
Guided Meditation

In my live and online Breakthrough to Success program, I lead the participants through a guided meditation to discover their life purpose.* (We will explore the power of meditation and mindfulness more fully later, in Chapter 12.) This meditation allows you to tap into the intuitive and creative aspects of your mind. We have included this meditation for you at jackcanfield.com/workbook-resources.

Step 1: Find a quiet place where you won't be disturbed for at least 20 minutes. Have a pen and paper nearby. Bring your Internet-connected device. Listen to the meditation now.

Step 2: If you received a gift during the life-purpose meditation, draw a picture of the gift below. If you have crayons or colored pencils, draw the gift in color.

Step 3: Describe that gift and what you think it means in terms of your life purpose.

_____

_____

_____

_____

_____

* This meditation, and others, is also available on the audio program *Awakening Power: Guided Visualizations & Meditations for Success* at JackCanfield.com.

WAIT! BEFORE PAUSING OR GOING FURTHER, DO THIS:

Write a brief description of the gift in *Your Life Success Journal* in the back of the Workbook on page 221. Then return here.

THE JOY REVIEW

Those things that bring you the greatest joy are in alignment with your purpose.

When you're experiencing joy, it indicates that what you're doing and how you're being are on purpose. It's like the GPS in your car or on your phone letting you know that you're on the correct route. Otherwise, it tells you to make a U-turn. When you go back and review the experiences of your life, and look for what brought you the greatest joy, you begin to get a sense of what your purpose is.

DISCOVERING MORE ABOUT YOU:
The Joy Review

Set aside about 20 minutes to go back over your life and make a list of all the times you felt the most joy. What were you doing? How were you being? You can record them below.

_____

_____

_____

_____

_____

_____

_____

_____

_____

_____

_____

_____

_____

_____

_____

_____

_____

_____

ALTERNATIVE JOY REVIEW

Here's another variation on the same exercise. To begin to hone in on your life purpose, make a list of five moments when you were doing something that brought you joy. To be most useful, you can state these activities in the present tense by completing the phrase, *I feel the most joy when I'm . . .*

Examples:

I feel the most joy when I'm *spending time with my children.*
I feel the most joy when I'm *creating a plan to expand my business.*
I feel the most joy when I'm *teaching others new leadership skills.*

Your turn:

I feel the most joy when I'm _____.

I feel the most joy when I'm _____.

I feel the most joy when I'm _____.

I feel the most joy when I'm _____.

I feel the most joy when I'm _____.

Now, look at what you wrote and see if you can find a pattern. Are two or more of them a similar type of activity? Write that activity below. Do that once more for the remaining activities. For me, one of the patterns of my joyful times is when I'm teaching. The second one is when I'm leading.

Joyful activity _____

Joyful activity _____

WAIT! BEFORE PAUSING OR GOING FURTHER, DO THIS:

Write your current version of your life purpose statement in *Your Life Success Journal* in the back of the Workbook on page 222. Then come back here for the conclusion of the life purpose discovery process.

DISCOVERING MORE ABOUT YOU:
The Life Purpose Exercise

While the meditation, The Joy Review, and the Alternative Joy Review will help you discover your purpose, this exercise is a simple but powerful way to create a compelling Life Purpose Statement. Take the time now to complete this exercise.

1. **What are two unique personal qualities that you most enjoy expressing in the world?** *
   Your unique qualities are strengths that are natural and easy for you to express, such as love, joy, enthusiasm, passion, authenticity, curiosity, transparency, creativity, courage, humor, generosity, kindness, patience, peacefulness, perseverance, and wisdom.

   _____   _____

2. **List two ways you most enjoy expressing those qualities when interacting with others, such as *supporting* and *inspiring*.** Other ways might include: writing, speaking, coaching, empowering, mentoring, singing, dancing, painting, leading, managing, inspiring, nurturing, protecting, healing, solving problems, building a business, inventing, traveling, creating, organizing, and integrating.

   _____   _____

   ### WAIT! Are You Reading This Exercise, But Not Doing the Work Required?

   Sometimes it's easy to just keep reading or scanning the next section to get to the "new stuff." Remember, this is a workbook, designed for you to actively apply these principles in your life. Grab your pen or pencil and complete each exercise fully in order to move toward the success you long for. If you don't have the time or desire to do this now, put the book away and come back when you are ready.

3. **Assume the world is perfect right now. What does this world look like?** How is everyone interacting with everyone else? What does it feel like? This is a statement, in present tense, describing an ultimate condition, the perfect world as you see it and feel it. Remember a perfect world is a fun place to be.

   Example of my perfect world: *Everybody is fully living their highest vision of their life, one in which they're doing, being, having, and experiencing everything they want.*

---

*There are several ways to approach defining your purpose. We learned this version of the life purpose exercise from Arnold M. Patent, ArnoldPatent.com.

Other examples might include: *Everyone is taking 100% responsibility for their own lives . . .* or *Everyone is living an ecologically sustainable lifestyle . . .* or *Everyone is living in peace and harmony with everyone else.*

_____

_____

_____

4. **Combine the answers to the three prior questions into a single statement.**

   Example: *My purpose is to use my creativity and enthusiasm to support and inspire others as we all freely express our talents in harmony, love, and joy.*

_____

_____

_____

5. **Check your life purpose statement in terms of the two guidelines mentioned earlier:**
   (a) Is it a single sentence? If not, you can consolidate it below.
   (b) Can you easily memorize it? Shorten it, if needed.

_____

_____

_____

6. **How does your life purpose statement look to you? Do you want to revise it further? If so, use the spaces below.**

_____

_____

_____

WILL YOU KNOW WHEN YOU HAVE DETERMINED YOUR PURPOSE?

Maybe. On the other hand, you may need to try it on for a while. Soon you may find yourself saying, *Yes, that is what's really important to me.*

You may think that what you wrote seems too obvious to be as special as your *life purpose.* You may even think, *Everyone probably has a similar one.* But if you're thinking that, don't be misled! It may seem common to you, but it is uniquely yours. The fact that it has always been true for you may make it seem ordinary.

The test is to ask yourself, *Is this what's truly important to me?* When your answer is yes, you'll know you've landed on it. It may be that your newly discovered life purpose statement is like a new pair of jeans that you need a bit of time to feel comfortable in.

ARE YOU THINKING, *I CAN'T LIVE MY PURPOSE, GIVEN MY SITUATION?*

Do you see obstacles in your life situation preventing you from fully living your purpose? Is it finances, family circumstances, your job, or something else?

If this is what you see, then take 100% responsibility for it, and change your situation! Your happiness, fulfillment, and success are at stake. Here are two approaches.

APPROACH #1: BE RESOURCEFUL AND CREATE YOUR OWN FUTURE

Brainstorm and then research ways that you can live in alignment with your purpose and incorporate those into your life, here and now—or at least very soon.

Here is how one woman solved this problem for herself.

When Julie Marie Carrier was a child, she loved animals. Adults around her would say, "Julie, you should be a vet!" When it came time for college, she enrolled in the pre-vet program at Ohio State University. She was lucky enough to spend her senior year in England, away from family and faculty. As she studied more of the sciences, she came to a stunning realization: *I'm totally miserable. I don't want to be a vet!*

She began to reflect on this, and finally asked herself, *What is a job I would love so much that I'd do it for free but that I could actually get paid for?* Julie thought back over all the things she'd done in her life and what had made her the most happy. Then it hit her—it was the youth leadership conferences that she had volunteered at, and the communications and leadership courses she had taken. With decisive action, she changed her major, and upon graduation, became a senior management consultant in leadership training and development for the Pentagon—all by the time she was 23! But that's not the end. She started speaking at events for kids all across her home state, and then went on to launch a new career as a public speaker on leadership and character. She had found her joy, and then created a life—and a livelihood—around her purpose.

APPROACH #2: MAKE YOUR PURPOSE MORE INCLUSIVE

Until you see yourself as able to change your circumstances, state your purpose in a more inclusive way such that you can do it almost anytime or anywhere. Remember, you can bring joy, inspire others, create beauty, or make whatever contribution you want based on your purpose—no matter where you are and no matter what you are doing.

That's why I wrote my purpose statement as *to inspire and empower people to live their highest vision in a context of love and joy in harmony with the highest good of all concerned*. I can do that anywhere—and I have. For example, I can be *on purpose* while I'm on my way to the airport, speaking with a complete stranger, the Lyft driver. I didn't state that my purpose was only to write books, give talks, or conduct trainings. I do those activities as a way of expressing and living my purpose, but I can live my purpose of inspiring and empowering people no matter where I am and no matter whom I am with.

FIREWORKS

When determining one's life purpose, some people expect fireworks to go off and their knees to weaken. This rarely happens. For many, it's a feeling of subtle satisfaction rather than one of explosive ecstasy. It may be a calm feeling of settling into something that seems right. It can be like looking for a pair of jeans that fit well. They may not feel perfect at first, but long-term they work well. Or you may immediately feel a sense of recognition of something that has always been there for you. The difference is that now you have put these feelings into words.

WHAT IF YOU CAN'T DETERMINE YOUR PURPOSE?

Some people can have a difficult time landing on a single life purpose statement, even after completing these exercises. In that case, consider what you come up with as a first draft, and start using it. Then revisit these exercises after a couple of weeks.

Wherever you are with your life purpose statement, I recommend you simply accept what you have for now. You can always revise it later. But just for now, drive a stake in the ground and declare to yourself that, yes, this is your life purpose statement.

Allow yourself to feel satisfied. You have determined (or begun to determine) your life purpose! You now know so much more about the true source of joy and fulfillment in your life. You now know what to focus on in order to have success come more easily to you with fewer struggles.

KEEP YOUR PERSONAL NORTH STAR VISIBLE

When sailors use the North Star for navigation, they have to actually look at it! To use your life purpose for guidance, you have to look at that, too. Keep your purpose visible, as I do. Right now, I look up and my purpose statement is written and posted right in front of me, on my desk.

HOW FULLY ARE YOU LIVING YOUR LIFE PURPOSE?

Answer the following question in the space below. On a scale of 1 to 10 (10 being highest), how fully are you living your life purpose on a day-to-day basis? If the answer is not a 10, write down what you could do to live your purpose more fully.

_____

_____

_____

_____

_____

_____

CONCLUSION

Sometimes our experience of life can seem like we are a small boat in the vast ocean. There are so many currents and winds trying to push us this way or that. There are so many directions we could follow, and so many choices we could make. Yet, something feels different once you're clear about your life purpose. You have identified your own North Star, your own Rock of Gibraltar. You now know what gives you joy and fulfillment in life. The more you do things aligned with that purpose, the more satisfying your life will be, and the easier it will be to achieve the success you want. You are now ready to experience all the fulfillment and passion and rewards you deserve from a life well lived.

LIVE YOUR PURPOSE

This is the true joy in life, the being used for a purpose recognized by yourself as a mighty one; the being thoroughly worn out before you are thrown on the scrap heap; the being a force of Nature instead of a feverish selfish little clod of ailments and grievances complaining that the world will not devote itself to making you happy.

GEORGE BERNARD SHAW
Nobel Prize–Winning Playwright

MAKE-IT-A-HABIT WORKSHEET
Keep Your Purpose Alive

Below are practical and easy action steps with which you can keep your purpose visible and alive each day.

Select the ones you will do and place a check mark ☑ next to them.

After you have checked off the ones you will do, put them on your calendar or add them to your to-do list so that you're reminded later to actually do them.

1. ☐ **Memorize your life purpose.** Use whatever technique you use when you have to memorize something critical, such as writing it down several times or creating a word association. Instead of posting your life purpose statement on your bathroom mirror, post only this prompt: My purpose is . . . By verbally filling in the blank a few times, you will have it fully memorized.

2. ☐ **Read your life purpose statement every morning and every night.**

3. ☐ **Create a document on your computer** with your life purpose statement that also includes a picture of you, then frame it and keep it on your desk or bedside table.

4. ☐ **Take a picture of your life purpose statement** with your smartphone and use the picture as the home screen on your phone or computer.

5. ☐ **Type up your life purpose in a creative and attractive style.** Print multiple copies and post it where you will see it, such as your bathroom mirror, your refrigerator, and your car dashboard.

6. ☐ **Make this a part of your morning routine:** Each morning, set your smartphone timer for two minutes. During that time, reflect on your life purpose. Think about how you can live it more fully—remembering the joy you feel when you're participating in those activities that are aligned with your purpose.

7. ☐ **Meditate about your purpose regularly.** We'll cover meditation in *Chapter 12*, but for now, follow these simple instructions: Spend a few quiet minutes alone, where you won't be disturbed. Take a few deep breaths, allow yourself to become relaxed, and enter a state of self-love and peacefulness. Reflect on what your purpose means to you, and what your life will be like as you live even more fully on purpose. Allow any images and ideas to come to you. Let this visual journey be as expansive as you can imagine.

8. ☐ **Tell the world!** Talk about your life purpose with those special friends who understand or want to know what you're about.

9. ☐ **If you're artistic, draw or paint a symbol or picture** that represents your life purpose.

10. ☐ **Clip pictures from magazines and create an image of you** living your life on purpose.

11. ☐ **Add your life purpose statement to the bottom of your email signature.**

12. ☐ **Write down your own idea.** Other ways you can keep your purpose alive for you:

_____

13. ☐ **Write down your own idea.** Other ways you can keep your purpose alive for you:

_____

14. ☐ **Write down your own idea.** Other ways you can keep your purpose alive for you:

_____

Great! Now put the ideas you checked above on your calendar or add them to your to-do list so that you're reminded later to do them.

Add to Your Life Success Journal

Turn to page 222 in *Your Life Success Journal*. You will see several questions to answer about your purpose statement. Go ahead and do this now.

DECIDE WHAT YOU WANT: ENVISION YOUR IDEAL LIFE

I am focused on what I truly want for my life
based on my own values and life experiences.

AFFIRMATION

What is the vision you have for your life? What do you really want? What does success look like to you? What would you pursue with passion if you knew you couldn't fail?

In this chapter, you'll have the chance to envision your best life, and then write it down. This may be the first time you've ever taken the time to do this—to dream big about what you truly want to be, do, and have.★

Take a moment now to recall one of your dreams for your life. See yourself in that ideal situation. Let yourself feel those wonderful feelings. It is those feelings, and the possibility of those dreams coming true, that help fuel your journey toward the success you want. Success happens when your dreams are authentically what you want and big enough to inspire you to take action to make those dreams a reality. Knowing clearly what you want is critical to success.

WERE YOU BROUGHT UP TO DREAM OR TO FOLLOW DIRECTIONS?

If you were lucky growing up, you were encouraged to dream big about who you wanted to be when you grew up, and what you wanted for your life. For many of us, though, our dreams were ignored, or we were told they were silly, or worse,

---

★If you haven't already, read *Principle 3: Decide What You Want* in the book *The Success Principles* for more explanation, stories, and examples.

that we would never amount to much. Many of us put aside what we wanted in order to get along or to avoid conflict. As we became adults, we were told to be practical and realistic. That worked for a while.

But what if you want more? While you may have had to adapt to survive back then, now you know that more is available to you. This is your chance to break free of any negative childhood conditioning and adult "being practical." Now is your time to expand your sense of yourself, to dream once more, and to envision what you truly want in all areas of your life.

DO YOU FEEL UNCOMFORTABLE WHEN ASKED WHAT YOU REALLY WANT?

Some people become uncomfortable when asked what they really want. Does this describe you? If so, maybe you've been asked before what you really want and you had no clear answer. Perhaps it brings up painful reminders of dreams you once had, but you feel you had to give up because they were out of reach. For others, dreaming big may feel embarrassing, unrealistic, or too self-focused. If any of this is true for you, now is the time to shake off any hesitancy or shame and boldly answer the questions that follow in this chapter. Remember, you have an innate right to dream and to pursue whatever you want! It is time for you to fully explore what the life you truly long for looks like.

HOW I LEARNED TO VALUE MY "WANTS"

An event years ago changed my life forever in this area. On the first day of a seminar I attended, I noticed a yellow notebook on my chair. Other seats had other colors. I don't like yellow—I wanted a blue notebook. Then the instructor said something that I remember to this day: "If you don't like the color notebook you have, trade with someone else and get the one you want. *You deserve to have everything in your life exactly the way you want it.*" Her words proved to be a turning point for me. Since then, I allow myself to tune into, to own, and to pursue what I really want—and to continue to expand my vision.

Do you feel stuck with the "yellow notebooks" in your life that you don't really want? Is there something you've been accepting or tolerating, not realizing that something better is actually available to you? What is it you would really prefer instead? What are the "blue notebooks" you want in your life?

WHY VISION IS SO IMPORTANT

It's the possibility of having a dream come true that makes life interesting.

PAULO COELHO
Author of *The Alchemist*

Deciding what you want is a key foundation block for building the life you want. You wouldn't build a home without a clear picture of what you want it to look like, would you? When you write down what you want, as clearly as you can, your brain receives specific images to work toward, both consciously and unconsciously. Having this clear vision will guide your actions and your decisions, as well as keep you motivated along the way. That's why I encourage you to dream as big as you dare to. You may be familiar with the following beautiful quote from Marianne Williamson. Read it twice, taking it all in. Notice if your sense of self and what is possible for you expands.

Our deepest fear is not that we are inadequate. Our deepest fear is that we are powerful beyond measure. It is our light, not our darkness, that most frightens us . . . Your playing small does not serve the world. There is nothing enlightened about shrinking so that other people won't feel insecure around you.

MARIANNE WILLIAMSON
Author of *A Return to Love*

Now is your time to imagine your best possible future. On the pages that follow are worksheets that address the most important areas of your life. When you think about what you want in each area, really go for it! Write down your heart's desires. Give yourself permission to list anything and everything that you want. Build your "I want" muscle. No one else needs to approve what you write—or even see it. This is for *you*. Dream big.

YOUR FINANCES

How much money do you want to have in the future? How much do you want to have invested when you retire? How much annual income do you want to make? If you're an entrepreneur, how much net profit would you like your business to earn? How much do you want in your bank account or in your investment portfolio? What do you want your net worth to be?

Don't limit yourself in this area. This is an exercise in developing your most inspiring *vision* for your life; this is *not* goal setting. No one is going to hold you accountable. This is your chance to light your inner fire. Remember, it takes no more energy, effort, or time to dream big than to dream small.

For now, don't worry about how you'll achieve what you want; the "how" will be addressed later. Right now, just focus on the "what."

Before beginning the exercise, read each word in the list below, and allow yourself to envision what you really want. Imagine how good it will feel to have what you want regarding your finances. Allow yourself to feel excited about your vision for yourself.

Warm up by thinking about . . .

Your ideal income. How much do you really want to be making every year?
Your ideal net worth . . . now and in the future.
Eliminating all your debt and being debt-free.
Your savings and investments. How much do you want, by when?

Now, grab your pen or pencil and complete the worksheet on the next page.

FINANCES
Income, Profit, Net Worth, Investments, Debt Reduction

What I Want

List what you want in the areas of income, profit, net worth, investments, debt reduction, cash flow, or other finances:

_____

_____

_____

_____

_____

_____

_____

_____

_____

_____

_____

_____

_____

_____

_____

_____

_____

_____

_____

_____

_____

_____

_____

My Reason Why

For each item you listed on the left, write down *the reason* that each of them is important to you.

_____

_____

_____

_____

_____

_____

_____

_____

_____

_____

_____

_____

_____

_____

_____

_____

_____

_____

_____

_____

_____

_____

_____

COULD YOU PRACTICE "10X THINKING"?

The value of thinking big is that it encourages you to go beyond your conditioning—to go beyond your everyday expectations for yourself and beyond what you think is possible. Here is your chance to go even further, using the same ambitious standard that Google tried to reach. According to their vice president of finance, the company encourages big thinking about its new products: For any new product in development, the goal is for the product's benefits to be "10X" or 10 times higher than the product or service it's designed to replace. That's a high standard—and we can apply it to our own lives! How about trying it yourself?

Consider this a thought exercise. It is a way to expand your thinking about what you want. It can expand your view of what might be possible. There is no real risk here.

But be ready: For some people, *10X Thinking* is an exhilarating process. For others, stretching in this way may produce some anxiety. You might feel tense, or foolish, or you may want to close the workbook and do something else. Whatever your response, it is OK. Just accept it for what it is: the natural response for you.

10X THINKING

If I **multiplied by 10** the most important numbers I wrote on the *Finances* worksheet, they would be:

My Income

_____

_____

My Profit

_____

_____

My Net Worth

_____

_____

My Investments

_____

_____

My Debt Reduction

_____

_____

My Cash Flow

_____

_____

My Other Finances

_____

_____

YOUR WORK, CAREER, OR BUSINESS

Whatever work you're doing now, do you love it? Is it what you truly want to do? What would your life look like if you were able to make your life's work doing what you truly love?

Most of us need to work in order to sustain our lives at the level we want. We're brought up expecting to work—either inside or outside the home—for most of our adult lives. Luckily, we all have a choice in the type of work we do—and in the level of satisfaction it brings us.

Think about your own career or business possibilities. You might want to find more joy and ease in your current work. Perhaps you want to find a new job in your field, or switch careers, or be self-employed, or do creative work, or raise your children full-time, or train horses, or pursue nonprofit or charitable work. Whatever it is, if you want to work at what you truly love to do, the process starts with envisioning and writing down what you truly want.

Warm up by thinking, if you could do anything you want, anything at all . . .

What would a career based on your life purpose look like?

What would you most love to do as your work, profession, or business?

What would be some characteristics of your ideal work environment?

Do you want to have a support team?

Do you want to be part of a collaborative team?

Do you want to work from home, or in a particular city?

WORK • CAREER • BUSINESS
Ideal Job, Purposeful Work,
Own Your Own Business, Work from Home

What I Want

List what you want in the area of your work, career, or business:

My Reason Why

List *the reason* why each is important to you:

YOUR RELATIONSHIPS

While work takes up a third of the day for many of us, relationships add richness to our lives. Relationships include those connections you have with your spouse or partner, family, extended family, close friends, colleagues at work, and members of the community. How satisfying and rewarding do you want these relationships to be? What new relationships do you want to bring into your life? What relationships do you need to modify or eliminate from your life? What do *you want* from your relationships?

Get started by thinking about an ideal relationship with . . .

    Your spouse or partner
    Your children
    Your siblings and extended family
    Your new friends
    Your long-time friends
    Your neighbors
    Your colleagues at work
    Members of your community

RELATIONSHIPS
Spouse or Partner, Children, Friends, Neighbors, and Colleagues

What I Want

List the relationships (and quality of relationships) you want in your life:

My Reason Why

List *the reason* each is important to you:

_____   _____

_____   _____

_____   _____

_____   _____

_____   _____

_____   _____

_____   _____

_____   _____

_____   _____

_____   _____

_____   _____

_____   _____

_____   _____

_____   _____

_____   _____

_____   _____

_____   _____

_____   _____

_____   _____

_____   _____

_____   _____

_____   _____

_____   _____

YOUR HEALTH AND FITNESS

If you were in charge of a factory or a school, you would likely have a manager in charge of the "physical plant." That includes the maintenance of the structures, the heating and ventilation, and more. Well, your body is your "physical plant." How well do you want it to operate and for how long?

Start by thinking about . . .

Your ideal weight
Your desired level of fitness or strength
Your level of flexibility (can you touch your toes?)
Your level of energy
The quality and length of your sleep
The quality of the food you eat
Remaining disease-free
The age you would like to live to

HEALTH AND FITNESS
Weight, Fitness, Flexibility, Energy, Sleep, Food, Life Span

What I Want

List what you want in the area of health and fitness:

_____

_____

_____

_____

_____

_____

_____

_____

_____

_____

_____

_____

_____

_____

_____

_____

_____

_____

_____

_____

_____

_____

My Reason Why

List *the reason* each is important to you:

_____

_____

_____

_____

_____

_____

_____

_____

_____

_____

_____

_____

_____

_____

_____

_____

_____

_____

_____

_____

_____

_____

YOUR FREE TIME, FUN, AND RECREATION

All work and no play is no fun at all. How do you want to balance your life with enjoyable or relaxing things to do? What gives you satisfaction and pleasure simply by the act of doing them? What activities would you like to take up or spend more time doing?

Consider . . .

Hobbies
Socializing
Gardening
Travel
Vacations and getaways
Music and the arts
Movies and comedy
Reading
Sports
Dancing

FREE TIME, FUN, AND RECREATION
Hobbies, Vacations, Entertainment, Travel, Sports

What I Want

List what you want in the area of free time, fun, and recreation:

My Reason Why

List *the reason* each is important to you:

YOUR PERSONAL AND SPIRITUAL GROWTH

Because you are going through this *Workbook*, it is clear that you are interested in your growth. What might it look like if you could have more of the personal growth you desire? What issues would you want to resolve? What is your ideal view of yourself as a person? Are you interested in growing spiritually? What about more education or professional skills? Are there things you want to do just for the experience?

Here are some ideas to prompt your thinking of what you might want to do . . .

Begin a new self-development practice, such as yoga or meditation

Attend a specific personal-growth workshop

Earn an advanced degree or certification

Take time for prayer

Go rock climbing

Take up downhill skiing

Coach a youth team

Join a group—or form a group

Adopt a morning routine

Write regularly in a journal

Start a blog

PERSONAL AND SPIRITUAL GROWTH
Professional Certification, Personal Development, Spiritual Practice

What I Want

List what you want in the area of personal and spiritual growth:

My Reason Why

List *the reason* each is important to you:

YOUR POSSESSIONS

We live in a world of amazing abundance! You can see examples all around you of beautiful homes, designer clothes, and elegant jewelry. You can see more when you watch TV or a movie, or visit upscale stores. It makes you realize the quality of possessions that are available to make your life more beautiful, more comfortable, and more enjoyable. So, what are some of the specific things that you want in your life? What do you want to have?

Think about . . .

Your ideal home, how big it is and where it is located

That great car or truck you want

A vacation cabin or a motor home

A specific television or sound system

A special watch, a beautiful ring, or other jewelry

Designer clothes, shoes, or accessories

A sailboat or fishing boat

A horse or an airplane

A set of power tools

A new computer, printer, or camera equipment

POSSESSIONS
House, Car, Clothes, Jewelry, Art, Recreational Vehicles

What I Want

List some of the possessions that you want to own or have access to:

_____

_____

_____

_____

_____

_____

_____

_____

_____

_____

_____

_____

_____

_____

_____

_____

_____

_____

_____

_____

_____

_____

My Reason Why

List *the reason* why each is important to you:

_____

_____

_____

_____

_____

_____

_____

_____

_____

_____

_____

_____

_____

_____

_____

_____

_____

_____

_____

_____

_____

_____

MAKING A DIFFERENCE AND BEING OF SERVICE

When you determined your purpose in *Chapter 2*, did it include a way in which you want to contribute to others, to a cause, or to the planet? Review your purpose now for consideration here. Beyond that, in what ways do you want to make a difference? Do you want to be of service, perhaps in your community? Is there a problem you want to help solve? A contribution you want to make? A legacy you want to leave?

Start by considering . . .

Does community service fulfill you?

Is there a group in need that calls to you?

Is there a contribution you long to make?

Do you want to leave a legacy (monetary or otherwise), and if so, what would it be?

If you could make a difference, what would it be?

MAKING A DIFFERENCE • CONTRIBUTION • SERVICE
Volunteer Work, Purpose Fulfillment, Legacy

What I Want

List the way in which you want to make a difference, contribute, or be of service:

_____

_____

_____

_____

_____

_____

_____

_____

_____

_____

_____

_____

_____

_____

_____

_____

_____

_____

_____

_____

_____

_____

My Reason Why

List *the reason* why each is important to you:

_____

_____

_____

_____

_____

_____

_____

_____

_____

_____

_____

_____

_____

_____

_____

_____

_____

_____

_____

_____

_____

_____

GREAT JOB!

You've finished creating a vision for your ideal life. Feel free to come back to these worksheets and expand or change your vision at any time.

For now, take a breath, relax, and acknowledge yourself for your work imagining your ideal future. This exercise can be challenging—it takes emotional energy as well as determination to get through it all.

Are you ready to keep your vision top of mind and make it a reality? Being clear about what you want is fundamental to taking steps to make it happen. The *Make-It-a-Habit* worksheet that follows will help keep your vision an ongoing part of your life.

MAKE-IT-A-HABIT WORKSHEET
Keep Your Vision Alive

Below are action steps that will not only help you keep your vision alive in your mind's eye—they'll help you to constantly create goals around the specific things you want to be, do, and have. Of course, as you grow and achieve your goals, your vision will likely change over time. That's perfectly fine. However, this original vision document—with changes or not—is something to always have near you, for as long as you desire a positive future. Treasure what you have written. This is your recipe for the ideal life and success you desire. We will do more work with your vision in the chapters that follow, using the tools of a vision board, affirmations, goal setting, taking action, believing it's possible, and more.

To make each new step a habit, put a check mark in front of each item below as you complete it.

1. ☐ Select the most important items from each of the eight areas of "wants." Write these in *Your Life Success Journal* on page 223 in the back of this workbook, under *Keep Your Vision Alive*.

2. ☐ Create a Word doc or a handwritten note with the headings of the areas you just completed, including finances, relationships, and the others. Add a line or two of what you want most in each area. Post it where you will see it to remind yourself each day.

3. ☐ Spend a few quiet minutes to breathe, become relaxed, and enter a state of deep self-love and peacefulness. Reflect on what your vision means to you, and on what your life will be like as that vision becomes your reality. Allow any images and ideas to come to you. Let this "visual journey" be as expansive as you can imagine.

4. ☐ Select a day of the week when you will review your vision. Put a recurring reminder on your calendar for that date. Sit down for 10 minutes to review and update your vision. (Can you spend more time on your vision each week? Of course. By setting a minimal 10 minutes, you are more likely to actually do it each week.)

5. ☐ Schedule a recurring one-hour appointment with yourself at the end of the year to fully review and revise your vision. Notice that, as you put this date on your calendar, you may feel relief that you are serious about applying what you are learning in this *Workbook*—confirming to yourself that this will not be an effort that is soon forgotten.

6. ☐ Include a two-minute reflection on the key elements of your vision as part of your morning routine.

7. ☐ If you have a meditation practice, meditate on your vision regularly. If you have not learned to meditate, I will provide instruction in a later chapter.

8. ☐ Tell others! Talk about your vision for your life with special friends who support you.

Add to Your Life Success Journal

If you haven't already, turn to *Your Life Success Journal* on page 223 and complete the exercise.

USE THE POWER OF GOAL-SETTING TO ACHIEVE YOUR VISION*

*The greatest danger for most of us is not that our aim is too high
and we miss it, but that it is too low and we reach it.*

MICHELANGELO
One of the Greatest Artists of All Time

In the previous chapters, you discovered your life purpose, and you clarified your vision of the success you want. Now it's time to take the necessary steps to make that vision your reality.

One reason many people don't achieve their vision is that they don't turn their vision into a set of specific goals. Until you write specific and measurable goals, your vision is too vague. For example, you might say you would like to have a new car, but you need to specify precisely *what* kind of car you want and exactly *by when* you expect to own it. Otherwise, your vision remains a dream, a nice idea, and just wishful thinking.

But this *Workbook* isn't about wishful thinking; it's about applying proven principles of success in order to get the results you want.

You're probably already aware of the concept of goal-setting. Yet, while nearly everyone has heard of goals (and some even set goals at work), very few people use goal-setting to get what they want in their personal life. Most people simply go to work, do what the boss says, then come home and watch TV. Not you. Not any longer.

I want you to be the exception—part of the 3% of people who take goal-setting seriously, who actually use it, and who, as a result, outperform everybody else. Setting goals is the crucial next step that will help you achieve the success

---

*Read *Principle 7: Unleash the Power of Goal-Setting* in the book *The Success Principles* for more explanation, stories, and examples.

you want. For any area of your life where you want to make a change or acquire something you want to have, you need to create a goal. Without a specific, written goal your chance of success is significantly reduced.

In this chapter, you will set goals for the vision you created in the previous chapter. You will also be guided to create a *Breakthrough Goal*—a goal that can be a game-changer for you. A Breakthrough Goal is one that will take you to the next level—and it will require you to grow and develop yourself to achieve it. In fact, as you'll soon learn through the exercises in this chapter, that resulting personal growth is one of the most exciting and fulfilling payoffs of setting goals.

I can never be safe; I always try and go against the grain. As soon as I accomplish one thing, I just set a higher goal. That's how I've gotten to where I am.

BEYONCÉ KNOWLES-CARTER
American Singer, Actress, and Fashion Designer

INCREASING THE ODDS OF ACHIEVING YOUR GOALS

Research conducted by Dr. Gail Matthews of Dominican University and Dr. Stephen Krause from Harvard★ identified ways to increase the odds of reaching your goals. They wanted to test the premise that people who write down specific goals for their future are more likely to be successful than people who either have unwritten goals or no goals at all. They recruited 267 participants from a variety of businesses and organizations and asked them to set business-related goals for themselves for an upcoming four-week period.

The participants were then randomly assigned to one of five groups, and each group was instructed to use one or more of the following supportive activities:

1. Simply think about your goals.
2. Write down your goals.
3. Make a list of actions you commit to taking toward your goals.
4. Send the list of the goals and the actions to a supportive friend.
5. Send a weekly progress report of your results to a supportive friend.

★G. Matthews (2007). *The Impact of Commitment, Accountability, and Written Goals on Goal Achievement.* Paper presented at the 87th Convention of the Western Psychological Association, Vancouver, B.C., Canada.

The first group was told to do only the first item: to think about their goals. For each of the remaining groups, the researchers added one additional type of support until the final group, Group 5, was told to apply all five. The table below shows the results each group obtained: the *Success Rate* indicates the percentage of goals reached by each group at the end of the study.

	Group 1	Group 2–3	Group 4	Group 5
Think about goals	✓	✓	✓	✓
Write down goals		✓	✓	✓
Share with a friend			✓	✓
Weekly **progress report** to friend				✓
Success Rate	43%	56%	64%	76%

This research provides substantial evidence that, in addition to just thinking about your goals, three "best practices" will help ensure you reach your goals. In fact, when you do these three things—in addition to taking action on your goals—your chance of success is much, much higher:

1. Write down your goal.

This is a must! There is no other option. Until you write down your goal, it is just an idea in your head. You need to make it more substantial, more real, and more grounded by putting words on paper (or writing them digitally).

What you write is also critical. Your goals need to be both *specific* and *measurable*. That is, you need to state "how much" and "by when."

For example, *I want to make more money next year* does not specify how much more you want or precisely by when you will achieve it. A specific version, on the other hand, would state it clearly: *I will increase my after-tax income to $140,000 by December 31st of next year.*

2. Tell a friend about your goal.

Find a supportive friend or colleague and tell them your goal(s). When you do this, you make the goal more real for yourself. You're making a declaration, and you're putting it out into the universe. It also deepens your commitment to the goal when you state your goal publicly.

Does the thought of telling someone about your goal scare you a bit? That's a good sign. It means you are stepping up to something bigger, and you are putting your reputation at stake, which will strengthen your motivation to accomplish it. Trust yourself, and go for it.

3. Set up a regular system of accountability, then report your results to a friend, colleague, coach, or mentor on a consistent basis.

One of the most powerful tools you can use to help you take steady action toward your goal is to ask someone to be your "accountability partner." This requires that you get their agreement, then tell them what you will do to report to them (and how often). It's best if you can find someone who is committed to achieving their own goals so that you can hold each other accountable. A word of advice, however: Don't recruit your spouse or life partner to be your accountability partner. It works better if you do this with someone you are not in a romantic relationship with in order to avoid turning accountability reporting sessions into an experience where you end up judging and nagging each other.

What does *regular and consistent* accountability look like?

"Every Friday by 5:00 p.m., for the next three months, I will email you and tell you whether I met my goal of calling on three new clients that week."

Knowing you'll be reporting your results to someone else carries a social consequence that is often enough to keep you motivated. Many people select a friend, and if you are feeling light-hearted, you can call them your "accounta-buddy." It could also be a work colleague, a coach, an accountability partner, or someone in your mastermind group. There will be more information on each of these alternatives in later chapters.

Often times, there are obstacles, distractions, and reasons to procrastinate that get in the way of reaching our goals. Having an accountability partner provides the extra motivation to tip the balance in your favor. After all, if your goals were easy to accomplish, you would have already achieved them.

BEST PRACTICES FOR WRITING A GOAL: INCLUDE "HOW MUCH" AND "BY WHEN"

The way you write your goals also makes a difference. Vague, nonspecific goals don't give you a basis for taking action, and they don't help you determine whether you've achieved the goal or not.

That's why it's critical to *be specific* and include two important elements in your goal: *how much* and *by when*. Without these elements, a goal is just too vague for anyone to know whether you have reached it or not. In addition, without clear specifics, your subconscious won't know exactly what it is that you want and won't be able to help you get it.

How much means writing a specific, measurable quantity, such as the number of pages written, number of pounds gained or lost, the amount of money earned, the number of square feet for the house you want, or the number of points you will earn.

By when means the exact time and date you want to achieve the goal—at the latest—so there's no question about the deadline.

Goals that are specific make a difference. If buying a car is your goal, include the make, model, color, year, and features. If you want to lose weight, instead of saying *I want to lose 10 pounds*, it is more powerful to say *I will weigh 135 pounds or less by 5:00 p.m. on June 30th of this year.* This makes it crystal clear.

You can test how well you have written your goal by asking yourself whether an outside observer who shows up at the time of completion could independently determine if you had reached your goal or not.

Remember, vague goals produce vague results.

GOOD IDEAS VS. SPECIFIC GOALS

Good ideas are vague. But specific written goals state in clear language the end result you are working toward.

A Good Idea	Written as a Goal
I want to own a home on the ocean.	I will own a 3,600-square-foot house on Shoreline Street in Portland, Maine, by 12:00 noon, April 30th of next year.
I want to start my own business.	I will launch my new business with a business license and a Web site by 5:00 p.m., September 15th of this year.
I want to lose this extra weight.	I will weigh 134 pounds or less by my birthday, November 17th, of this year.
I want to be more kind and positive with my children.	I will say something positive to each of my children at least once a day for the next 30 days.

THE PURPOSE OF GOAL SETTING IS LIFE MASTERY

The real purpose of using goals to pursue what you want goes well beyond just acquiring "stuff"—a fast car, that beautiful house, the dream job, plentiful money, or whatever it may be for you. The fact is, even after you achieve these things, any one of them could disappear in a moment—through a bad investment, a business bankruptcy, a fire at your home, or an unexpected illness.

But there's one thing that can't be taken away: *your newly gained knowledge, confidence, and ability* to produce results whenever you want.

That's the biggest payoff of setting and achieving goals. In fact, if everything you've accomplished all went away in an instant, you could reproduce it all over again. That is the state of *mastery*.

TURNING YOUR VISION INTO GOALS

Write Goals to Support Your Vision

Now is the time for you to write down those goals that will make a difference in your life. You will select goals that will move you closer to your vision of the life of your dreams. Turn to *Your Life Success Journal* on page 223 of this *Workbook*. Find what you wrote down that you most want in each of the eight areas of your vision from *Chapter 3*. If you're going to achieve your vision in each of these areas, ultimately you are going to have to set a goal for each one.

Keep These Points in Mind

1. **Set three goals**. If you are new to goal setting, you might want to start smaller and build success by setting **only three goals** from among the eight areas. As you accomplish these goals, you can then set more goals to make your vision a reality. The reason I suggest starting with only three goals is to ensure you don't overwhelm yourself. Over time, you will learn how to calibrate the size and quantity of goals for yourself. You want to find the balance between it being a motivating stretch for you and having a reasonable likelihood of success.

   If you are a veteran goal-setter, you may want to set one goal for yourself in each of the eight areas as a way to create an overall balanced and fulfilling life.

2. **Start by setting goals that can be achieved in one to three months:** The duration for each goal should be around 1 to 3 months. That length is long enough to have a benefit and short enough for you to have a taste of success. After that, you can set a new goal based on what you have learned about yourself and what it takes to reach that goal.

Create a Specific and Measurable Goal in at Least Three Areas of Your Vision

Take a look at these examples:

Area of Your Vision	Goal (How Much, by When)
Finances	I will increase my commissions by 15% (to X dollars) by June 20th of this year.
Health & Fitness	I will exercise for at least 30 minutes a day, five days a week, Monday through Sunday until November 15th of this year. Exercise includes running, walking, yoga, or other forms of exercise that get me moving.
Relationships	By the end of this month, I will research and identify five individuals, in priority order, who could mentor me in growing my business, and within the next 30 days I will contact them one by one and secure at least one new relationship that permits two coaching calls per month.

Now it's your turn. Remember to use the guidelines for writing specific goals by stating *how much* and *by when*.

Area of Your Vision	Goal (How Much, By When)
1.	
2.	
3.	

Ready to keep going and create goals for all eight areas of your vision? Turn to page 224 in *Your Life Success Journal* and write the remaining goals you need to work on achieving.

CREATE A BREAKTHROUGH GOAL

If you want to be happy, set a goal that commands your thoughts, liberates your energy, and inspires your hopes.

ANDREW CARNEGIE
One of the Richest Americans in History

Now that you've written at least three goals to turn your vision into reality, you are well on your way to getting the life you want. But what if you want to play a bigger game? You might be ready to go for it, to stretch and grow, and do all you can to create the life and success you desire. If this describes you, then consider setting a Breakthrough Goal.

What Is a Breakthrough Goal?

- It's a goal that is an ambitious stretch for you.
- It's a goal that is big enough to produce a *quantum leap* in the area of life you select—your finances, career, health, or relationships—such that your life will never be the same once you achieve it. In other words, it's a goal that will amplify your life in every area.
- It's a goal that you can accomplish in one year.
- Your Breakthrough Goal should be very compelling for *you*. Just the idea of accomplishing it must be so motivating that it will inspire you when you face challenges.
- You will know you are on the right track if the Breakthrough Goal you choose scares you somewhat when you think about taking it on.
- You are on the right track if you aren't exactly sure just *how* you will be able to accomplish the goal. It will require that you learn to trust that the "how" will show up. Think of it as throwing a stake in the ground, far beyond your current reach.

Here are some examples of breakthrough goals that my students have set and accomplished for themselves.

- Double my income
- Get 20 new clients for my coaching practice
- Start my own business
- Hire a personal assistant
- Launch my own podcast
- Write and publish a book
- Open up China as a market for my network marketing business
- Appear on Oprah's *SuperSoul Sunday* television show
- Get a consulting contract with Apple, Google, or Microsoft

Has an idea for a Breakthrough Goal just occurred to you? If so, grab that inspired idea and write a draft of it on a separate piece of paper or in your journal. If not, no worries. There is more to come.

You may have heard about interviews with older people who are reflecting on their long life and are asked about whether they have any regrets. Consistently, they mention regrets about things they *failed to do*—not things they *actually did*. With that in mind, you have the opportunity right now to avoid any such later disappointments.

Is there something you have always wanted to do, be, or have, but haven't yet pursued? Make a note of it here.

_____

_____

There is also solid research that shows that when one sets a big goal, the results are also big. Edwin Locke, Gary Latham, and their associates reviewed all studies that were conducted over an 11-year period about goal-setting.* They found that when the goals were ambitious and specific, the results produced were *actually higher* than the original goal 90% of the time compared to the results produced when the goals were not very ambitious. Here is the takeaway: Setting goals works. Setting bigger goals works better. This is one more reason to stretch, to risk, and to go after what you want in a big way.

Choose a Breakthrough Goal that will take you to the next level and that will require you to grow and develop as a person in order to achieve it. Remember, the real benefit is who you become in the process.

Step-by-Step Process for Creating a Breakthrough Goal

1. If you made a note earlier about a possible Breakthrough Goal, write it here. If not, take another look at what you wrote when you determined your vision in *Chapter 3*. What did you say you wanted and wrote down in *Your Life Success Journal* on page 223? List three of the most important ones here.

_____

_____

_____

*E. A. Locke, K. N. Shaw, L. M. Saari, and G. P. Latham. (1981). "Goal Setting and Task Performance: 1969–1980." *Psychological Bulletin*, 90(1), 125–152.

2. Circle one item you wrote down above that most inspires you and is most important to you.

3. Now that you've selected the area—whether it's finances, career, health and fitness, or another area—what is the *specific, measurable result* you most want that would create a significant breakthrough in your life?

_____

_____

4. By what date and time will you produce this result? (Maximum time is one year from now.)

_____

5. Review what you wrote. Do you need to make any changes to this Breakthrough Goal? Write your final version of your Breakthrough Goal here.

_____

_____

Congratulations! You did it. You are one big step closer to becoming a master of your own life, just by identifying and committing to your Breakthrough Goal.

You may notice that just by writing down that goal, with the intention for it to become your reality, that you already feel different—a little more positive about yourself and your future.

As you work toward making your Breakthrough Goal a reality over the next year, remember to keep encouraging yourself, as you go full out and become the master of your life.

MAKE-IT-A-HABIT ACTIVITIES

1. Keep your goals visible by rereading your goals regularly.
2. Carry a list of your most important goals with you, perhaps in your wallet where you can see it, such as behind the plastic where your driver's license usually is.
3. In the next chapter, you will learn to use visualizations and affirmations to help bring about your goals even faster.

MAKE-IT-A-HABIT WORKSHEET
Keep Your Goals Alive

In the chapters that follow, you'll learn powerful ways to reach your goals, including strengthening your belief in yourself, creating a vision board, using affirmations, taking inspired action, and much more. Below are some action steps for you to implement right away—they will help you to keep your goals alive day-to-day.

Choose the steps you will take from the list below. As you implement each one, put a check mark in front of the item.

☐ Tell others. When you make your goals public by sharing them with friends, family, and colleagues, they become more real to you.

☐ Keep track each week of your progress on your goals.

☐ Ask a friend or colleague to hold you accountable. Tell them how often you will report your results to them, such as a daily or weekly text, email, or phone call.

☐ Post your goals on social media.

☐ Set a timer on your smartphone that repeats each day and label it with your goals.*

☐ If you write in a journal, write about your goals and your progress.

☐ Rewrite your goals on a regular basis, such as making it part of your morning routine.

☐ Take a digital picture of your goals list, and display it on your computer desktop.

☐ Type your goals into a notes app or document software and print multiple attractive copies.

☐ Post your goals where you will see them daily, such as:

   ☐ In your wallet, right next to your money

   ☐ On your car dashboard

   ☐ On your bathroom mirror

   ☐ On your refrigerator

   ☐ Taped to the edge of your computer monitor

   ☐ In a picture frame on your desk or your bedside table—or both

---

*On an iPhone, open the *Clock* app and tap the *Alarm* tab at the bottom. Tap the "+" sign in the top right corner. Set the desired time for your new alarm. Tap *Label*, and write a short reminder of your goals. Tap *Repeat*, and select the days you want to be reminded of your goals.

On an Android smartphone, open the *Clock* app. Tap the *Alarm* tab on the upper left-hand side. Tap the "+" sign on the lower right-hand side. Tap the *Date* icon on the right side to select the start date. Tap *Done*. Enter the time for the alarm. Select the *Days* for the alarm by tapping on the name of the days you choose. For alarm *Name*, write a short reminder of your goals. Tap *OK*.

Add to Your Life Success Journal

Turn to page 224 of *Your Life Success Journal* and complete the exercises for this chapter.

CHAPTER

5

USE AFFIRMATIONS AND VISUALIZATIONS

*I never hit a shot, not even in practice, without having a
very sharp, in-focus picture of it in my head.*

JACK NICKLAUS
PGA World Record-Holder, Author, and Philanthropist

Two of the most underutilized tools for success are affirmations and visualizations. Together they greatly accelerate the achievement of any success you desire by harnessing the amazing power of your subconscious mind.

In this chapter, you will learn to create and use affirmations in the correct way to accelerate the achievement of your goals. You will create an affirmation for at least three of the goals you set earlier, plus one for your Breakthrough Goal. Then twice a day you will repeat the affirmations and combine them with a visual scene of your completed goals to activate the creative powers of your subconscious mind.

You will also learn how to create a Vision Board using pictures, symbols, graphics, and words representing your dreams and goals. I will give you suggestions for where to post it to get the maximum value and impact from it.★

HOW AFFIRMATIONS HELP YOU GET
WHAT YOU WANT IN LIFE

Affirmations are vividly detailed statements of you living, working, and enjoying life *as if your goals had already been achieved.* Affirmations help your brain focus on bringing about your heartfelt desires.

★ Read *Principle 11: See What You Want, Get What You See* in the book *The Success Principles* for more explanation, stories, and examples.

I'm happily depositing my first $100,000 royalty check as a bestselling author is one example of an affirmation. *I'm joyfully receiving the company's top sales award* is another.

How do affirmations work?

As scientists now know, the brain is a goal-seeking organism. If you give it a compelling, colorful, crystal clear image of what you want, it will work night and day to create the opportunities, contacts, resources, and circumstances needed to achieve that vision. In fact, the brain has a special function called the *reticular activating system* that filters through the millions of impressions, images, messages, and thoughts it processes each day and passes to your conscious mind that specific information that will help you reach your goal.

For example, if you've thought about speaking at your industry convention as a way to boost your career, then immediately remembered you met the National Education Director last month at a trade show, that's your *reticular activating system* bringing you ideas and contacts that can help you achieve your goal.

HOW TO WRITE AFFIRMATIONS FOR YOUR UNIQUE GOALS

Affirmations are the way to focus your brain on the goals you want to achieve. Writing them out on index cards, note cards, your smartphone's wallpaper, on a sign at the bottom of your bathroom mirror, or in other places you see frequently is a way to constantly focus on your most important goals. Use the guidelines below to write powerfully effective affirmations for your unique situation—using your notes about what you want to be, do, and have:

1. **Start with the words "I am."** Your subconscious mind interprets these two powerful words as a command—they are the most effective words in our language.
2. **Use the present tense.** Describe what you want as though it has already been accomplished.
3. **State it in the positive.** Don't think about what you don't want—affirm what you *do* want.
4. **Keep it brief.** Think of your affirmation as an advertisement slogan—make it short enough to be easily remembered.
5. **Make it specific.** Vague affirmations produce vague results.

6. **Include an action word ending with -*ing*.** The active verb adds power by evoking an image of doing it or experiencing it right now.

7. **Use at least one dynamic emotion or feeling word.** Include the emotional state you would be feeling if you had already achieved the goal, such as: *enjoying, happily, celebrating, proudly, peacefully, enthusiastic, lovingly,* and *triumphant.*

8. **Make affirmations for yourself, not others.** Construct your affirmations by describing your behavior; it has nothing to do with someone else.

Here is a simple form for affirmations that includes all the guidelines above that you can use to quickly and easily create affirmations that work:

I am so happy and grateful that I am now _____.

An example would be: *I am so happy and grateful that I am now earning $100,000 a year.* Or *I am so happy and grateful that I am now at my ideal weight of 135 pounds.*

USING AFFIRMATIONS TO ACCELERATE ACHIEVING YOUR GOALS

It's easy to use affirmations as a tool for achieving your goals. Simply review your written affirmations in the morning when you first wake up, then at night just before you fall asleep. You don't always have to know *how you'll accomplish the goal*; just keep visualizing yourself in the future, *as if you had already achieved it.*

Add color, sounds, emotions, and other sensory aspects to your visualization time—the feeling of confidence as you deliver the keynote address at your industry's annual conference, the scent of cinnamon rolls baking at the bed-and-breakfast hotel you recently opened, the sound of the waves breaking at the senior executives retreat in Hawaii, the joy you feel as you're living out your dream career or professional accomplishment.

MY AFFIRMATION STORY

When I was younger, I didn't believe in the power of affirmations and visualization—until I gave them a try. Now I am a believer because I experienced the benefits in every area of my life. You are going through this workbook because you want a higher level of success. Well, now is the time for you to take a leap of faith and apply these powerful tools.

Here is what I did over 40 years ago and how it worked out for me. At the time, I was working hard and making about $25,000 a year (about $103,000 in today's dollars). Not bad, but I wanted to be much more successful than that. I wanted to make four times as much—or more.

Here's the affirmation I used: *I am happily and easily earning, saving, and investing $100,000 a year.*

But affirmations alone—just the words—are not enough. You need to add images, too. Affirmations and visualizations work together to produce a combined effect that will radically change your future. The more senses you engage, the better—it helps make it as real as possible. So be sure to include the sounds you would hear and, most important, the emotions you would be feeling as you go through your day with your goal achieved. The positive feelings you generate at the thought of your success will keep you motivated to continue to take the necessary actions toward your goals.

Once I decided on my affirmation, I also created an oversized replica of a $100,000 bill, and I taped it to the ceiling, right above my bed.

Each morning when I woke up, I would see the bill, then close my eyes and repeat my affirmation, *I am happily and easily earning, saving, and investing $100,000 a year.*

I imagined just what it would be like to enjoy my $100,000-a-year lifestyle. I envisioned the house I would live in, the furnishings and the artwork in it, the car I would drive, and the vacations I would take. Then I focused on the feelings I would experience once I had attained that lifestyle. I dove fully into those feelings! It was as though I was already there.

Did this work for me? Before I tell you about my results, I want to explain *why* this works.

STRUCTURAL TENSION OCCURS IN YOUR SUBCONSCIOUS MIND

When you say to yourself that you are enjoying what you have achieved, even though it is not yet your reality, it creates what is called *structural tension* in your subconscious. Your brain wants to close the gap between what you are saying and seeing in your mind—and what is your actual current reality. By continually repeating and viewing your goal as already achieved, you are increasing this structural tension. Your brain wants to resolve the tension and get back to equilibrium—so it stimulates the creative aspect of your mind to find solutions, and expands your awareness of the resources around you (that you were previously not seeing), which can help you close the gap and achieve your goal.

By repeating the affirmation and visualization each day, your subconscious starts to buy into the idea that you've already achieved the result. The structural tension builds, with your brain saying, "Okay, we get it. She's not going to give up on this. So to get her to stop bombarding us with this tension every day, we're going to have to produce what she wants."

Your subconscious begins to constantly focus on how to get you to your goal.

About a month after I started focusing on the image of that $100,000 bill over my bed—then repeating my affirmation and closing my eyes and visualizing my $100,000-a-year lifestyle each morning—I got my first breakthrough idea of how to make more money. I kept getting more ideas and took action on each one. By the end of that year, I had generated an income of $92,325 vs. the $25,000 I had earned the year before—not exactly $100,000, but trust me, I wasn't complaining. In fact, that $92,325 in today's dollars would be a whopping $356,000—a huge change in my family's lifestyle. The results were so impressive that my wife asked, "If affirmations work for $100,000, do you think they would work for a million dollars?"

So, I made a new affirmation—*I am happily depositing my million-dollar royalty check from my bestselling book.* I added images and repeated the affirmation twice a day, along with focusing on the intense feelings of how great it would be to have that check for $1 million. I achieved that goal, too, and have continued to earn $1 million or more every year since.

> *Create a vision for the life you really want,*
> *and then work relentlessly towards making it a reality.*
>
> ROY T. BENNETT

WRITE AN AFFIRMATION FOR EACH OF YOUR GOALS

Step 1: Write Down Your Goals

Turn to the previous chapter starting on page 69. There you'll find the three goals (or more) you wrote based on your life vision. Write each one in a space below labeled *My Goal #1, #2* and so on.

Step 2: Write an Affirmation for Each Goal

Now, in the spaces indicated, write an affirmation for each of your three goals, plus one for your Breakthrough Goal, using the eight guidelines on pages 76–77.

This example will give you an idea of what an affirmation looks like:

My Goal #1: *I will weigh 124 pounds or less by 8:00 p.m. on December 31st of this year.*

My Affirmation for Goal #1: *I am so happy and grateful that I now have a healthy and fit 124-pound body.*

Step 3: Write a Statement to Help You Visualize

Now that you've written an affirmation for each of your goals, create an image in your mind of your life once you have achieved that goal. Imagine as many details as you can—your lifestyle and activities, sights, sounds, and emotions. Make notes of the features to remind yourself later using the spaces provided. As you visualize these images day after day, the entire scene will easily come back to your mind for each goal. In fact, you'll see your future as though you're merely watching your life on a television screen—changing channels as you move through your goals.

This example will give you an idea of what a visualization statement looks like:

My Visualization Statement for Goal #1: *I see myself on the scale looking down, and it reads 124 pounds, and I hear myself cheering excitedly. I walk over to the mirror and see my firm, healthy body. My spouse hears me and runs in and says, "Congratulations!"*

Now Let's Get Started on Writing Your Affirmations . . .

My Goal #1: _____

_____

My Affirmation for Goal #1:

I am so happy and grateful that I am now . . . _____

_____.

Identify the sights, sounds, and emotions you will focus on as you recite this affirmation. What will you be feeling once your goal is achieved? Then write a statement to help you visualize.

The activities and daily lifestyle I see in my future: _____

_____

The sounds and scents I'm experiencing in my future: _____

_____

The emotions I am feeling now that my goal is achieved: _____

_____

My Visualization Statement for Goal #1: _____

_____

_____

_____

_____

My Goal #2: _____

_____

My Affirmation for Goal #2:

I am so happy and grateful that I am now . . . _____

_____.

Identify the sights, sounds, and emotions you will focus on as you recite this affirmation. What will you be feeling once your goal is achieved? Then write a statement to help you visualize.

The activities and daily lifestyle I see in my future: _____

_____

The sounds and scents I'm experiencing in my future: _____

_____

The emotions I am feeling now that my goal is achieved: _____

_____

My Visualization Statement for Goal #2: _____

_____

_____

_____

My Goal #3: _____

_____

My Affirmation for Goal #3:

*I am so happy and grateful that I am now . . .*_____

_____.

Identify the sights, sounds, and emotions you will focus on as you recite this affirmation. What will you be feeling once your goal is achieved? Then write a statement to help you visualize.

The activities and daily lifestyle I see in my future: _____

_____

The sounds and scents I'm experiencing in my future: _____

_____

The emotions I am feeling now that my goal is achieved: _____

_____

My Visualization Statement for Goal #3: _____

_____

_____

_____

Locate your Breakthrough Goal on page 72 of the previous chapter and write it here.

My Breakthrough Goal:_____

_____

My Affirmation for My Breakthrough Goal:

I am so happy and grateful that I am now . . . _____

_____

Identify the sights, sounds, and emotions you will focus on as you recite this affirmation. What will you be feeling once your Breakthrough Goal is achieved? Then write a statement to help you visualize.

The activities and daily lifestyle I see in my future: _____

_____

The sounds and scents I'm experiencing in my future: _____

_____

The emotions I am feeling now that my goal is achieved: _____

_____

My Visualization Statement for My Breakthrough Goal: _____

_____

_____

_____

_____

Imagination is everything. It is the preview of life's coming attractions.

ALBERT EINSTEIN
Winner of the Nobel Prize in Physics

REPEAT YOUR AFFIRMATIONS AND
VISUALIZATIONS TWICE A DAY

Remember, your affirmation and your visualization need to be linked together—and done together each day. Repeat your affirmations with your visualizations *at least twice a day.* (The best times are when you first wake up and right before you go to bed. And if you meditate every day, do them immediately after your meditation.) Make sure to write the times into your daily schedule. It's also a good idea to put a reminder on your bathroom mirror.

Commit to this schedule and continue until you reach your goal. The more you affirm and visualize your goals, the more likely and the more quickly you will achieve the success you want. All the while, you will be basking in the good feelings that come from experiencing this positive future for yourself.

CREATE YOUR VISION BOARD

A Vision Board uses pictures, symbols, graphics, and words to represent what you most want to achieve—your dreams and your goals. We are visual creatures, and we respond to what we see. You have probably heard the expression "Seeing is believing."

To create your Vision Board:

- Use pictures from magazines, brochures, catalogs, or the Internet and make a collage on a poster board, door, or wall.
- Find pictures of people doing the things you dream of doing.
- Gather pictures of the places you want to visit or where you want to live.
- Find images of those things you want to own, such as a beautiful home, your dream car, or the jewelry and the clothes you want to own.
- Put yourself into the picture. For example,
  - If your goal is to own a Tesla, go to a dealership and ask the salesperson to take a picture of you sitting in the driver's seat.
  - If you dream of going to Machu Picchu in Peru, print a picture of Machu Picchu from the Internet and paste or Photoshop a picture of yourself into the scene.

- If you want to start or grow your business, mock up a cover of *Inc.* magazine with you on the cover—and make a great headline to go with it. Mark Victor Hansen and I created a mockup of the *New York Times* bestsellers list with the original *Chicken Soup for the Soul®* book in the number one spot. Within 15 months, that dream became a reality.

Here is an example of my vision board. You will notice I use a specially designed folding vision board.★

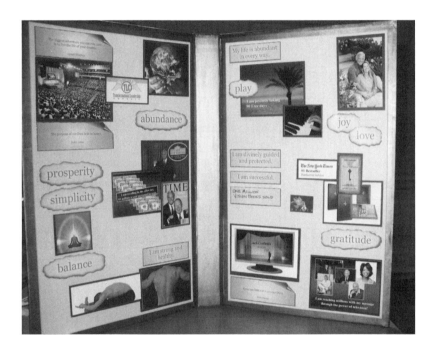

CREATE YOUR VISION BOARD

Take the time now to create your Vision Board of your dreams and your goals.

1. Obtain a poster board from a store that sells school supplies. If you prefer, you can use a large picture frame, a bulletin board, or your refrigerator door.
2. Gather several magazines with colorful pictures. You may have some on hand, or if you want a greater selection, many doctor and dentist offices dispose of their waiting room magazines each week.

★ These Vision Board kits are available for adults, teens, and children on my Web site at www.jackcanfield .com.

3. Flip through the magazines and clip pictures that match an aspect of your vision.

4. If you want more pictures or specific pictures, conduct an Internet search for images that meet your needs. In the search box, start with the words "images for . . ." and the search results will include pictures.

5. Print the pictures you found on the Internet. If you don't have a color printer, you can go to a copy shop to print them.

6. Assemble your Vision Board by affixing the pictures to the board in an attractive composition.

7. Add words that support or clarify your vision, such as *Vicky's Dream Home, #1 Salesperson, Love, Joy, Wealth, Abundance,* or *Happy Family.*

8. Hang or place your Vision Board where you will see it every day.

9. Each time you view it, take a moment to feel the feelings you think you will have when that vision is your reality.

10. If you are in a committed relationship or have children, it's a great idea to take an evening or time on the weekend, and have your partner or your whole family create your Vision Boards together.

11. You can also make a digital Vision Board that you can view every day on your computer, tablet, or smartphone. Check out the fantastic tool called Mind Movies at www.MindMovies.com.

The only thing worse than being blind is having sight but no vision.

HELEN KELLER
The First Deaf-Blind Person to Earn a BA Degree

MAKE-IT-A-HABIT WORKSHEET
Keep Your Affirmations and Visualizations Alive

Below are practical action steps you can take to keep your affirmations and visualizations visible and alive each day.

Select the ones you will do and place a check mark ☑ next to them.

After you have checked off the ones you will do, add them to your to-do list, or better yet, schedule them in your calendar so that you'll be reminded at the later time to do them.

1. ☐ Make your Vision Board. Follow the directions described earlier in this chapter.

2. ☐ When you pass by your Vision Board during the day, pause for at least 10 seconds, look at it, and feel what it will feel like when you have achieved the things you have envisioned.

3. ☐ Make a written copy of your affirmations for your bedside table. Repeat your affirmations and visualizations every morning and every evening.

4. ☐ Memorize your affirmations. You want to have your affirmations always available for you to repeat at any time or anywhere. Use whatever technique you have used in the past when you have had to memorize something important. Common methods include repeatedly writing out each affirmation 10 times or more a day or repeating each one to yourself out loud.

5. ☐ Take a picture of your affirmations with your smartphone and use the image as the home screen on your phone or computer.

6. ☐ Write your affirmations into the *Notes* app on your smartphone and read them during the day.

7. ☐ Write your affirmations on a card and keep it in your billfold, wallet, or purse where you will see it during the day.

8. ☐ Write your affirmations on an index card and tape it to your dashboard where you will see it often.

9. ☐ Embellish your visualizations. Review the notes you made and expand the visual images to make the power of your visualizations even stronger.

10. ☐ Record your affirmations and listen to them while you work, exercise, drive, or fall asleep.

11. ☐ Print your affirmations and put them in an 8x10-inch picture frame.

12. ☐ Hang duplicate pictures of items from your Vision Board around your house or apartment.

13. ☐ Repeat your affirmations during "standby time" such as waiting in line or when you are driving.

14. ☐ Repeat your affirmations when you exercise.

15. ☐ Repeat your affirmations in the first person, such as "I am . . . ," then in the second person, "You are . . . ," and in the third person, "He or she is . . ." or "(Your name) is . . ."

Don't underestimate the power of your vision to change the world.

LEROY HOOD
World-Renowned Scientist, Inventor, and Entrepreneur

Add to Your Life Success Journal

Turn to page 227 of *Your Life Success Journal* and complete the exercise for this chapter.

BELIEVE IT'S POSSIBLE*

You have to believe in yourself when no one else does. That's what makes you a winner.

VENUS WILLIAMS
Professional Tennis Champion

To achieve your breakthrough goal and the success you want, you first have to believe that it is possible for *someone* to do it. Then you have to believe that it is possible for *you* to do.

Belief is a necessary ingredient in achieving something—especially when it is something you haven't done before. The purpose of this chapter is to give you tools that will allow you to increase your belief in yourself dramatically. When you fully believe that it is possible for you to accomplish something new and big, you are much more likely to stick with it and find a way. When you believe, your conscious and subconscious minds then go to work to help you make it happen.

FIRST, BELIEVE IT'S POSSIBLE THAT *SOMEONE CAN DO IT*

To strengthen your belief, you can start by locating examples of others who have already done the thing that you want to achieve (or something similar to it). As humans, we are social animals; we learn from other people's experiences. While your Breakthrough Goal may be new for you, there are likely countless others who have already accomplished it or done something similar. It's well worth the

---

*Read *Principle 4: Believe It's Possible* and *Principle 5: Believe in Yourself* in the book *The Success Principles* for more explanation, stories, and examples.

investment of your time to find examples of people who have already accomplished what it is you are striving to achieve.

You can find great examples of other people's successes by reading their biographies and self-help books. You can also find stories of success that will inspire you and confirm your belief that ordinary people can accomplish extraordinary things in the following places:

- **Magazines**, such as *People, O (The Oprah Magazine), Entrepreneur, Inc., Wired, Fast Company, Sports Illustrated,* or *Success.*
- **TV shows**, such as Oprah's *SuperSoul Sunday, Shark Tank, 60 Minutes, Ellen,* or *CNN Heroes: Everyday People Doing Extraordinary Things to Change the World.*
- **Podcasts**, such as *How I Built This* with NPR's Guy Raz, about people who started companies in their parents' basement or their kitchen that later grew to become household names; *Eventual Millionaire* with business coach Jaime Masters; and *The School of Greatness* with Lewis Howes. For a longer list, Google "25 Must-Listen Podcasts For the Woman Entrepreneur," or something similar.
- **YouTube videos**, such as *Best Motivational Video for Success in Life with Denzel Washington,* or *5 Women Entrepreneurs Share Their Secrets to Success.*

You will discover examples of quite ordinary people who decided to believe they could accomplish something they wanted, did the necessary work, and became successful. When you see these examples, you expand your belief of what is possible for a person to achieve. Then you will be able to say with confidence that, yes, it is possible for someone to do this.

> *If my mind can conceive it, and my heart can believe it, then I can achieve it.*
>
> MUHAMMAD ALI
> World Heavyweight Boxing Champion

BELIEVE IT'S POSSIBLE THAT *YOU* CAN DO IT

Once you see that it is possible for *someone* to do it, you next need to believe that it is possible for *you* to do it. You need to conclude, "If they did it, then *I* can do it, too!" This belief is critical for your success. How do you get that level of belief? If there were a secret to self-confidence and to believing in yourself, it is this: Believing is a *choice*. Yes—you can *decide* that from this day forward, you are going to believe you can have the success you want and you can reach your Breakthrough Goal. You will only need to *decide* to believe you can do it.

Are you ready to decide? Now is the time.

- STOP HERE -

Pause your reading and make the decision, right now, to believe you can accomplish your Breakthrough Goal. Make that decision now, even though you might not yet have any idea about *how* you will achieve your goal. You don't need to know how yet; you just need to decide. Once you have made the decision—right now—to believe you can do it, continue reading.

- CONTINUE -

LIMITING BELIEFS

To keep your new belief alive, you need to identify and eliminate your old, limiting beliefs. Limiting beliefs are the thoughts that spring up when you think about what you want to achieve. They take the form of, "I want this, *but . . .*" Those "buts" are the limiting beliefs. These limiting beliefs are almost always false and are often formed in childhood or young adulthood when you were most impressionable. Your limiting beliefs might be based on something your parents, guardians, teachers, or peers told you. Or your limiting beliefs might have been what you told yourself when something negative happened to you.

The most common limiting beliefs are some variation of, "I'm not good enough." Or, "I'm not (fill in the blank) enough." These beliefs form the background of what you think about yourself and your capabilities. These beliefs get in the way of your going after almost anything you want—because you accepted the idea that it is not possible. Here is an example of how a limiting belief affected one woman, Catherine Lanigan.

When Catherine was young, she was considered an excellent writer. As a college freshman, she was invited to attend a creative writing seminar that was usually reserved for seniors. A visiting professor from Harvard, who was an imposing six-foot-six man in a tweed jacket and horn-rimmed glasses, was teaching the class. After reading her first story, he called her into his office and told her, "Your writing stinks!" She was devastated. He told her that her parents were wasting their money and that she needed to change her major. He offered a bargain. "I'll give you a B if you'll promise never to write again." She agreed.

Catherine didn't write for 14 years. But as fate would have it, she happened upon a group of journalists at a hotel pool once when she was out of town. Getting up her nerve, she approached them. "My secret dream was to be a writer," she said. An older man in the group turned to her. "Is that right? Because if you wanted to be a writer, you'd be writing."

She explained that she had it on good authority that she had no talent. The man said he believed that anyone could write and gave her his card, saying to contact him when she had written something.

That moment changed her life. Catherine realized she had held on to a belief that she was not talented and had no business writing.

She went home and wrote a book!

When she sent it to the writer she had met, he was impressed. He introduced her to an agent, and a contract was soon in the works. She began to have a new belief of what was possible, and she kept taking action.

To date, Catherine has forty titles to her credit. You may recognize two of the titles from the hit movies on which they were based, both starring Michael Douglas and Kathleen Turner—*Romancing the Stone* and *The Jewel of the Nile*.

Think about this for a moment: Catherine lost the first 14 years of what was to become a lucrative and creative writing career because she chose to believe it when someone else told her she couldn't write. Don't ever let someone else's comments limit you. Remember, your beliefs are a choice. Choose to believe in yourself no matter what anyone else says. Today, Catherine has new confidence in herself and about her writing. She says, "I will never give up my dream again. *Never!*"

HAVE YOU GIVEN UP ON YOUR DREAMS?

Are there dreams you have given up because you didn't believe it was possible for you to achieve them? Do the following beliefs ring any bells for you?

I'm too old.
I'm too young.

I don't have enough education.

I can't afford to do what I love.

I have to work at this job that I don't like because I need the money.

I can't change my marriage . . . my situation . . . my body . . . my health.

Or this all-too-common belief that keeps people from going after what they truly want: *People can't just go and do that!*

A lot of people think they can't achieve success because they didn't start young enough, or that they're too old. Sister Madonna Buder challenged that belief when she was in her mid-40s and living life as a nun. A priest suggested she take a run on the beach, saying that running harmonizes the mind, body, and soul.

Grabbing some shorts and a T-shirt out of a donated clothes pile, she began to run for the first time in her adult life. Less than 10 years later, she completed her first triathlon. Now, 4 decades later, at 89, she is known as the Iron Nun because she has participated in 340 triathlons and 45 full Ironman Triathlons. She has also been a star in Nike's *Unlimited* TV campaign, which you can find on YouTube.

Sister Buder has appeared in *People, Runner's World, U.S. News and World Report, Sports Illustrated*, and many more. She now holds the world record for the oldest woman to finish an Ironman Triathlon. Do you think you are too old to achieve what you want? Not a chance.

INSTALLING NEW BELIEFS

One way to overcome the impact of a limiting belief, once you become aware of it, is to create the opposite belief and affirm that new belief by repeating it to yourself (out loud if possible) several times a day. For example, if your limiting belief is *I'm too old to achieve my goal*, change it to *I am the perfect age to reach my goal*. If it is *I don't know enough to accomplish that goal*, change it to *I can learn everything I need to know to achieve my goal*, or *I can partner with the right people to achieve my goal*.

You can also use some of the general affirmations below to strengthen your belief in yourself and your abilities.

- *I am capable of achieving anything my heart desires.*
- *I confidently believe in myself and my abilities, whether or not anyone else does.*

- *I always expect the best, and I always get what I expect.*
- *I have everything I need to create anything I want.*
- *I am confidently and courageously confronting my fears and self-doubts and moving forward on my life's journey.*
- *I am comfortably asking for guidance and advice from those who know what I need to know.*
- *In life's marvelous journey, I know where I am and where I want to be.*
- *I am changing my thoughts, images, and behaviors to produce the results I want.*
- *I am acting in alignment with my life purpose, and therefore all my actions automatically serve others as well as myself.*

I suggest you repeat each affirmation you choose to use several times, and then go on to the next affirmation. You can also write out each affirmation several times. You can also record yourself saying each affirmation, and then play back the recording while you are doing what we call "hands busy–mind free" tasks such as washing the dishes, putting on your makeup, or exercising. One of my friends who was in the movie *The Secret* made a recording of his affirmations that plays the same affirmations over and over, and he listens to them on his iPod when he runs every day. He now makes a multimillion-dollar passive income every year.

Another way to quickly and easily replace your limiting beliefs with positive empowering beliefs for success is to purchase a copy of my *Maximum Confidence: 10 Steps to Extreme Self-Esteem* audio program. It is a digital MP3 download audio program, which utilizes a revolutionary new technology called the Tri-Sync Integration Process to bypass your conscious mind and easily and effortlessly install powerful new beliefs into your subconscious. You can get it on my Web site at JackCanfield.com.

SELF-CHECK:
Do You Believe It's Possible for You to Accomplish Your Breakthrough Goal?

The following exercises will help you to assess yourself.

1. **Write your Breakthrough Goal.** Turn to *Chapter 4: Use the Power of Goal-Setting to Achieve Your Vision* on page 62 of this workbook, and locate your Breakthrough Goal. Write it below starting with, "I believe it is possible for me to . . ."

_____

_____

2. **Rate how confident you are that it's possible for you to achieve this goal.** Choose a number from 1 to 10.

    1 = No, I don't believe that it is possible for me to achieve this goal.

    5 = Maybe it's possible.

    10 = Yes, I believe it is possible for me to achieve it.

Your 1–10 rating (Be honest!): _____

3. **If your rating was less than an 8, take steps to address your lack of belief.** Remember, belief is a choice. You have to decide right now that you can reach your goal. Stop for a minute and write down three things you can do to bring your belief up to 8, 9, or 10 within the next week. Examples include:

    • Each morning I will repeat my affirmations, and each day choose to believe I can achieve my Breakthrough Goal.

    • Each morning I will visualize myself accomplishing my goal, and I will restate my belief that, yes, I can do it!

    • Each morning I will repeat my "I believe" statement five times, with more confidence each time.

1. _____

_____

2. _____

_____

3. _____

_____

4. **Make a note on your calendar to do the above activities this week.** Don't worry about not knowing the "how" of reaching your goal. You can address that later. Achieving a breakthrough right now requires that you *believe* you can do it, even in the face of having no plan. Your willingness to believe is the magic that Walt Disney spoke of when he said, "If you can dream it, you can do it."

GIVE UP THE WORDS "I CAN'T"

Imagine getting rid of all those thoughts that detract from your belief in yourself. You may not realize it, but there is a hypnotic impact from speaking the words "I can't." If you are going to be successful in life, you have to give up the phrase "I can't." Using these words disempowers you. Thinking or speaking the words "I can't" has been shown to make you physically weaker when you think them or say them.

Think back to when you were very young, maybe two or three years old. You were beginning to explore the world. You thought you could do anything and you were unstoppable. Then, because of difficult, unpleasant, and traumatic experiences over your lifetime—and the conclusions and decisions you made in response to those experiences—you began to think you weren't capable of doing all the things you wanted to. You learned to say and believe, "I can't."

It's now time to change that early childhood (and later) programming. You need to remove—entirely—the words "I can't" from your vocabulary. Here's how.

Turn "I Can't" Into "I Can"

The purpose of this exercise is to reduce the power that "I can't" has over you by converting the statement to a more *accurate* one. Most often, when you say "I can't," it's a lie. What is true is a statement such as, "I haven't learned how to—yet." Or, "I don't want to."

Step-by-Step

Start by making a list of at least five "I can't" statements you find yourself saying frequently. It is especially useful to write down any "I can't" statements you say regarding accomplishing your Breakthrough Goal.

Examples:

I can't quit my job.

I can't save enough money.

I can't start my own business.

I can't build a successful team.

I can't find the time to write a book.

I can't find time to play with my children.

I can't find time to exercise.

I can't ask my boss for a raise.

Write five of your "I can't" beliefs below.

1. I can't _____.

   When I say that, I feel _____.

2. I can't _____.

   When I say that, I feel _____.

3. I can't _____.

   When I say that, I feel _____.

4. I can't _____.

   When I say that, I feel _____.

5. I can't _____.

   When I say that, I feel _____.

Once you have written each statement above, say it out loud, and notice how you feel. Make a note of this feeling in the space provided. Examples of these feelings might include, *When I say that, I feel weak . . . I feel hopeless . . . I feel sad . . . I feel stupid . . .* or *I feel like giving up.*

Next, rewrite each statement you wrote above, replacing "I can't" with "I won't."

1. I won't _____.

   When I say that, I feel _____.

2. I won't _____.

   When I say that, I feel _____.

3. I won't _____.

   When I say that, I feel _____.

4. I won't _____.

   When I say that, I feel _____.

5. I won't _____.

   When I say that, I feel _____.

Next, read each one of these new statements out loud. Notice if you feel different when making an "I can't" statement versus an "I won't" statement. Make a note of the feeling on the lines above. Remember, your feelings contribute to your motivation for success and this exercise will help you notice these feelings. Examples of these new feelings include, *When I say that, I feel hopeful . . . I feel more powerful . . . I feel more responsible . . . I feel like it is up to me . . . or I feel like I've been holding myself back.*

Are you ready to take it to the next level and forever eliminate your "I can't" statements? Using the spaces below, rewrite each statement above using "I will" instead of "I won't."

1. I will _____.

   When I say that, I feel _____.

2. I will _____.

   When I say that, I feel _____.

3. I will _____.

   When I say that, I feel _____.

4. I will _____.

   When I say that, I feel _____.

5. I will _____.

   When I say that, I feel _____.

When you're finished writing, say each statement out loud and notice how you feel as you make these new statements. Do you feel more in control of your life? Do you believe in yourself more than ever? Make a note of how you feel on the lines provided. Example: *When I say that, I feel unstoppable . . . I feel more motivated . . . I feel powerful . . . or I feel joyful.*

Here are two more quick techniques for eliminating the words "I can't."

1. Wear a rubber band on your wrist. Every time you say, "I can't," gently snap the band—not enough to hurt, but just enough to heighten your awareness and provide a minor negative stimulus.

2. Put a glass fishbowl in your home somewhere where you can always see it, such as in your kitchen or by the front door. Place another one somewhere at work. Every time you say "I can't," put a dollar in the fishbowl. You can also invite your family and your coworkers to join you—asking them to help by pointing out every time you say, "I can't." You will find that children especially love to catch adults when they say "I can't." After a month, your family or coworkers can decide where the money collected should be spent or donated.

MAKE-IT-A-HABIT WORKSHEET
Acknowledge Your Daily Successes With a Victory Log

A powerful way to increase your belief in yourself is to keep a written record of your daily successes in what is called a "Victory Log." Each evening, review your day and write down all the successes you have had that day. Keep a running list in a notebook, or a note-taking app on your smartphone such as *Notes*, *OneNote*, *Evernote*, or *Google Keep*.

By recalling and then writing down your successes each evening, you log them into your long-term memory, which enhances your belief in your ability to achieve goals and create success. You will begin to see that you have the experience and the self-confidence to achieve any goal you want again and again. And whenever you need a boost of confidence, you can reread what you have written.

Step-by-Step:

1. Decide where you want to create and keep your list, such as in a notebook, on your smartphone, or somewhere else.

2. Create your list with the title My Victory Log and the date at the top.

3. Each evening, write down your daily successes for that day. Your successes might include:

• Your accomplishments and achievements during the day.

• Any personal disciplines you kept, such as exercising, meditating, or reading.

• Any temptation that you did not give into, such as not eating dessert, not watching too much TV, or not drinking too much alcohol.

4. Read over what you wrote and acknowledge yourself fully. Allow at least 20 seconds for the good feelings of accomplishment to soak in.

5. Say to yourself, "If I could do that, then I can do _____ (insert your Breakthrough Goal or another goal)!"

MAKE-IT-A-HABIT WORKSHEET
The Mirror Exercise

One of the most powerful techniques I know for increasing belief in yourself—and one that I've been using myself for decades—is the Mirror Exercise. Every night before you go to bed, stand in front of a mirror, make direct eye contact with yourself, and verbally acknowledge yourself for all of your successes for that day, both big and small. The Mirror Exercise will quickly help you build your self-esteem and your self-confidence. This exercise is based on the principle that we all need acknowledgment, and the most potent acknowledgment we can receive is the acknowledgment we give to ourselves.

Step-by-Step:

1. Before you go to bed, find a quiet place where you can stand in front of a mirror.

2. Look into the mirror and maintain eye contact with yourself throughout the entire exercise.

3. Start by saying your name. Then acknowledge yourself for each success you had that day, each discipline you kept, and any temptations you resisted.

4. End by saying, "I love you." (I know that seems weird, but do it anyway.)
   Your Mirror Exercise might sound something like this:

   > *Jessica, I want to acknowledge you for finishing the first version of your new song, for working out for 30 minutes this morning, for asking Jonathan for more support in getting the new client project done on time, for eating a healthy lunch, for not spending hours on Pinterest after dinner, and for going to bed at a reasonable hour tonight.*

   Whatever you accomplished that day, acknowledge yourself for it. *And then add . . .*

   > Finally, I want to acknowledge you for sticking with the Mirror Exercise and acknowledging your successes tonight. I love you.

5. End the exercise by standing there for several seconds to fully feel the impact of this experience. After all, you are the one in the mirror who just received all this acknowledgment and appreciation. The most important thing during this last part is not to turn away from the mirror because you are feeling embarrassed or thinking of yourself or the exercise as stupid or silly.

I recommend that you do this exercise for the next 49 days in a row without missing one day and notice how it changes your life. You will find that thoughts of self-affirmation and self-validation are slowly replacing your negative self-talk. You may also discover that you want to continue doing this daily exercise for the rest of your life. One of my students has now done it for over 3,000 days (that's 8 years) without missing a day!

You can use the handy tool on the next page to keep track of your daily use of the Mirror Exercise. Use the grid to check off each day you complete your Mirror Exercise for 49 days. Duplicate this grid on a separate piece of paper or 3" x 5" index card and post it on the mirror where you will see it every evening.

S	M	T	W	T	F	S
1	2	3	4	5	6	7
8	9	10	11	12	13	14
15	16	17	18	19	20	21
22	23	24	25	26	27	28
29	30	31	32	33	34	35
36	37	38	39	40	41	42
43	44	45	46	47	48	49

MAKE-IT-A-HABIT WORKSHEET
Display Your Symbols of Success

The more you can view yourself as your own success story, the more likely you are to believe you can create even more success. Do you have items in your house that are symbols of your past accomplishments? Are the items stored away out of sight somewhere, such as in the garage, in a shoebox, or in a closet?

Do you have a degree or a certificate you could frame? If you wrote and published a book, do you have the cover displayed in an attractive frame? Do you have sports trophies or other diplomas, photographs, medals, awards, or letters of recognition?

You can display these as a way to continually remind yourself—both consciously and subliminally—of your ability to create results and manifest your dreams.

Step-by-Step:

1. Gather together all these symbols and images of your past successes.

2. Find a place where you can attractively arrange and display them so that you see them regularly—such as on a wall, a bookcase, or a shelf.

3. When you pass by this display, take a moment to acknowledge yourself for what you have accomplished.

Add to Your Life Success Journal

Turn to page 228 of *Your Life Success Journal* and complete the exercise for this chapter.

TAKE ACTION!*

You can't cross the sea merely by standing and staring at the water.

RABINDRANATH TAGORE
Winner of the Nobel Prize in Literature

You can't get from *where you are* to *where you want to be* without taking action. When you begin to take action toward achieving what you want, you trigger all kinds of things that will carry you to success. You let those around you know that you are serious in your intention. Others start to pay attention to what you are doing. People with similar goals become aligned with you. You begin to learn from your experience about what works and what doesn't. You begin to get valuable feedback about how to do it better, faster, and easier. Things that once seemed confusing begin to become clear. Your confidence expands, and you start to become more fully engaged in all areas of your life. You find yourself in the arena and not just a spectator in the stands.

TWO DIFFERENT KINDS OF ACTIONS

As you begin to think about the actions you will take in the pursuit of your goals, it is useful to understand two different kinds of actions: obvious actions and inspired actions. Both are important for your success.

Obvious Actions

Obvious actions are the practical steps that are required to accomplish the goal you have in mind. Examples of these actions include learning a specific skill such as real

---

*Read *Principle 13: Take Action!* in the book *The Success Principles* for more explanation, stories, and examples.

estate sales, completing a certification course such as for massage therapy, or creating a business plan for your new venture. You can discover the obvious actions that are required to achieve a specific goal by reading about, studying with, and interviewing those who have already achieved similar goals. You can also learn what you need to do from a coach or mentor with expertise in the area of your goals, or by conducting research online and in books for the best steps for accomplishing your goal.

Inspired Actions

Inspired actions are the actions you take as a result of inner guidance, intuitive insights, a hunch, or a gut feeling. Sometimes a great idea will come to you complete and in a flash. Other times, you may have a thought like, *I don't know why, but I have this urge to call a former colleague,* or *I'm just feeling a strong need to attend that conference.* Listen to these voices and follow your inner guidance.

There are many ways for you to create a fertile ground for these ideas to emerge, such as fully committing 100% to a goal, using visualizations and affirmations, and meditating on or praying about your goal. It's also a great idea to keep paper and a pen on your bedside table or nearby during meditation to capture these ideas when they come up. A good axiom to live by is "As soon as you think it, ink it." Otherwise, these subtle thoughts can easily disappear from your conscious awareness.

ADOPT A BIAS FOR ACTION

One of the biggest differences separating people who succeed from those who don't is that winners *take action*. If you want to learn to play the piano, you need to play the piano. *Taking action* is what makes the difference.

Ordinary people hesitate, often weighing things over and over in their mind forever. For you to achieve more than you have before, you need to take new actions and more action than you ever have before. As you take action, you learn more—and faster—than if you always wait and think about it. Many high achievers have said that their secret to success is to fail faster than anyone else—and the only way to fail is to take action by trying new things. Follow the advice from the top-selling brand of athletic wear: *Just do it!*

CHUNK IT DOWN

A journey of a thousand miles begins with a single step.
CHINESE PROVERB

As you discover all those actions that will be required for you to accomplish your Breakthrough Goal, it's possible you may feel overwhelmed. That is normal. The nature of any stretch goal is that it requires you to think bigger than you have been thinking and take new actions that you haven't taken before. Here's what works in this situation. Begin by chunking the big steps down into smaller tasks. That way, the first step, as well as each next step, will be easier to focus on and do. Breaking down a large goal into smaller tasks—and accomplishing them one at a time—is the only way a big goal gets achieved.

Writing this *Workbook* is an example of a big goal. Even for me, the idea of writing a new book, in addition to all the other work I am doing, can seem overwhelming. But what I have learned over the decades is that no matter how big the goal, breaking it down into bite-size chunks and working on them one at a time makes it so much easier. Here is how I chunked down this goal.

Goal: Create and Publish The Success Principles Workbook

Here are the action steps we took to plan the book, write the book proposal to present the idea to my literary agent, and ultimately write this *Workbook*, and get it published:

- Schedule the book's production on my annual calendar
- Plan the tentative content of the book as a companion guide to *The Success Principles*
- Locate my best previous book proposal to use as a template
- Write a compelling summary of the *Workbook* for the beginning of the proposal
- Create a table of contents for *The Success Principles Workbook*
- Write a brief chapter summary for each proposed chapter
- Update the marketing plan section of the old book proposal
- Update our coauthor biographies
- Submit a draft to my coauthors for their input
- Incorporate their suggestions

- Submit the proposal to my literary agent for her suggestions
- Incorporate her suggested changes
- Submit the proposal to my publisher
- Divide the research, writing, and editing work with my coauthors
- Submit the draft manuscript to the publisher
- Correct the publisher's queries and finalize the manuscript

Here is a motto I like to keep in mind when I am working on a big goal:

Success by the yard is hard; success by the inch is a cinch.

Another example of a goal that can seem overwhelming is running and completing a marathon. But once you chunk it down and identify smaller goals along the way, it becomes far less intimidating. First, to make it a Breakthrough Goal, select a race and date when you will run. Then break this big goal into smaller steps, or minigoals. Starting with the end in mind: For instance, how many miles do you need to run each month to prepare thoroughly for the race? You could say, "I'm going to run a minimum of three miles a day, six days a week for the first month." Then you can write down how much you will increase it by each month until you're ready for running the marathon on Race Day.

Chunk It Down Using Mind Mapping

Mind Mapping is a great tool that I use for chunking down my goals. It's also useful for brainstorming the various steps that will be required to reach your goal. Examples of *obvious actions* might include the information you'll need to gather, the people to interview, the skills you'll need to acquire, any budgets you'll need to create, as well as the necessary funding you'll need to obtain. It helps to have a method for brainstorming and organizing the various steps—and mind mapping was designed for generating to-do lists like this.

Note that Mind Mapping takes a nonlinear approach. That is, instead of trying to first come up with the needed actions in sequential order, it allows you first to think more randomly and yet capture the ideas in a way that you can later turn into a list of sequential action steps.

Start by taking a look at the example Mind Map below called "Launch My Podcast." It was created by drawing a large oval in the middle of the page, then writing the intended outcome or goal inside of it. In this case, the goal was to launch a podcast.

As research was conducted and experts were consulted, major benchmarks or action steps were identified—such as Budget, Marketing, and Funding—and a new spoke and circle were added to the Mind Map for each of these major categories of activity.

Of course, once these major categories are identified, individual action steps for each category can be researched, investigated, masterminded, discovered by asking, and clarified—and then written onto smaller spokes branching off from each category's circle.

The unique advantage of a Mind Map is that it allows you to capture ideas as you think of them—writing them in relation to other items—all without having to make a list in sequential order. Later, you can organize all the action steps into a logical order with beginning and completion dates, which can then be placed into your calendar.

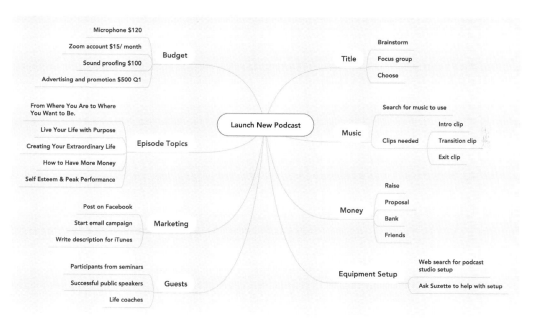

This Mind Map was created using the online tool at MindMeister.com. Some features are free; others require a fee.

Now, complete a Mind Map for your own Breakthrough Goal, or another important goal you've identified.

1. **Gather supplies:** Have at hand a large sheet of paper and a pen or marker. You can use 8.5" × 11" paper or, if you have access to larger sheets of paper, a

flip chart or large whiteboard is even better. With larger paper, you can add additional circles and have more room for branches and action steps. Or you can use a Mind Mapping program like Mindmeister.

2. **Draw your center circle:** In the middle of the page, draw a large circle, like the one in the example above. Make sure it's large enough for you to write your projected outcome inside of it.

3. **Write your desired outcome in the circle:** In the example above, the outcome is "Launch My Podcast."

4. **Draw each outer circle, as needed:** As you think of each category of tasks you'll need to complete in order to accomplish your goal, draw a spoke from the main circle and end it with a new, smaller circle. Write the name of the category inside this smaller circle. Take a look at the example above: these categories of tasks include *Budget, Episode Topics, Marketing, Guests, Title*, and so on.

5. **Draw spokes branching out from each new circle:** Along each of these individual spokes, write the task to be accomplished. When you're finished, you will have created a master list of actions to take.

6. **Transfer each task to a master chart, calendar, or project management software:** Organize all action steps into a logical order with beginning and completion dates.

MAKE-IT-A-HABIT WORKSHEET
Take Action for Your Success

You now have the most important action items in your Mind Map. The next step is to schedule them. Select a date when you will start each action and a date by when it will be completed. As an example, this first line was completed using the information from the Mind Map on page 105.

Actions I Will Take	I'll Start By	I'll Finish By	Done
Set a budget for the podcast.	*Sept. 22*	*Sept. 30*	✓

Now it's your turn. Add action items and dates.

Actions I Will Take	I'll Start By	I'll Finish By	Done
	/	/	
	/	/	
	/	/	
	/	/	
	/	/	
	/	/	
	/	/	
	/	/	
	/	/	
	/	/	
	/	/	
	/	/	
	/	/	
	/	/	
	/	/	
	/	/	

THE RULE OF 5

I learned this powerful lesson when Mark Victor Hansen and I published the very first *Chicken Soup for the Soul®* book. We interviewed several well-known, bestselling authors to find out what they saw as the "obvious actions" we would need to take to make the book a bestseller. We received an overwhelming list of suggestions. How were we going to implement all of the useful ideas from these experts?

We decided to seek the advice of Ron Scolastico, a wonderful teacher who taught us a life-changing lesson. He told us, "If you would go every day to a very large tree and take five swings at it with a very sharp ax, eventually, no matter how large the tree, it would have to come down." How simple and yet how true! From that advice, we developed what we called the Rule of 5. Every day we did at least five specific things that would move us toward reaching our goal of getting *Chicken Soup for the Soul*® to the top of the *New York Times* bestseller list. And by applying the Rule of 5, we did it! Not just once, but many times. Each day, we would make five requests for radio interviews or send five review copies to editors who might review the book, or call five network marketing companies to ask them to buy the book as a motivational tool for their salespeople, or call five churches to see if they would sponsor an evening seminar after which we could sell the book at the back of the room. Some days we would simply send out five free copies to influential people listed in *The Celebrity Address Book*—people such as Harrison Ford, Barbra Streisand, Paul McCartney, and Steven Spielberg. It was a lot of effort—a minimum of five things a day, every day, day in and day out—for more than two years.

Was it worth it? Yes! The first *Chicken Soup* book eventually sold more than 10 million copies in 43 languages. That is the power of the Rule of 5.

MAKE-IT-A-HABIT
Practice the Rule of 5

Practice the Rule of 5 with a daily "Top 5 Priority Actions" list. This is the simplest way to ensure that you are taking steady action in the direction of your goals and dreams. This daily list is crucial to planning and organizing the top actions that will have the greatest impact on your success. It will help you to stay focused and spend time only on those tasks that will reap you the greatest rewards—and help you eliminate other time-wasting activities.

Each evening, use your "Top 5 Priority Actions" list to plan your next day using questions such as:

• What action can I take to move closer to my Breakthrough Goal?
• What needs to happen tomorrow?

- Who should I call?
- What action from my Mind Map do I need to complete?

Reviewing your "Top 5 Priority Actions" list is an ideal way to start each day, knowing exactly what you should be doing.

I found the Rule of 5 to be so useful in our company that we printed up our own special Post-It Notes just for this purpose. These 3" x 3" square stickies come in a pad of 365 notes for daily use.★

TOP 5 PRIORITY ACTIONS

THE CANFIELD TRAINING GROUP
JACKCANFIELD.COM

Behind every great achievement, you will find a story of a person taking action and then more action. Anyone who wants success has to be willing to pay the price, regarding the time and effort required to achieve success. The people who have gone after and achieved what they have always wanted know that the effort and overcoming obstacles required is only temporary—while the benefits last forever.

Add to Your Life Success Journal

Turn to page 229 of *Your Life Success Journal* and complete the exercise for this chapter.

★ To order your own pad of 365 "Top 5 Priority Actions" Post-It Notes, visit JackCanfield.com.

CHAPTER

8

EVERYTHING YOU WANT IS ON
THE OTHER SIDE OF FEAR*

*I learned that courage was not the absence of fear, but the triumph over it.
The brave man is not he who does not feel afraid, but he who conquers that fear.*

NELSON MANDELA
Former President of South Africa and Nobel Peace Prize Winner

Whenever you start a new project or pursue your Breakthrough Goal, it's natural to have considerations, fears, and roadblocks. Considerations are negative *thoughts*, fears are negative *feelings*, and roadblocks are actual *obstacles* in the world you have to address.

Roadblocks include things like lack of money, lack of support (from your boss, colleagues, and family members), lack of knowledge, lack of connections, lack of free time to work on it, competitors, and other stopping points. These are real things that you have to address and that you may not have total control over. But what you *do have control over* is your fear, and that is what we're going to focus on in this chapter. As you move forward on your journey to success, you'll learn how to confront, to accept, and to overcome your fears.

Fear is something you'll most likely experience whenever you go after something significant you want to achieve. It's important to realize, though, that fear is something you can learn to effectively address so that you can take the actions that are needed to achieve your goals.

I think [being] fearless is having fears, but jumping anyway.

TAYLOR SWIFT
Singer, Songwriter, and Winner of 10 Grammy Awards

---

*Read *Principle 15: Experience Your Fear and Take Action Anyway* in the book *The Success Principles* for more explanation, stories, and examples.

Unfortunately, most people let fear stop them from taking the necessary steps to achieve their dreams. They are afraid they will fail, or lose money, time, reputation (or worse), or experience rejection or embarrassment.

Successful people, on the other hand, acknowledge their fear along with the rest of us, but they don't let it keep them from doing anything they want to do—or have to do. They understand that fear is something to be acknowledged, experienced, and either taken along for the ride or totally released. To be successful, you need to learn effective strategies for acknowledging your fears and taking action anyway.

THE VALUE OF FEAR

In days when we lived in caves and tribes, fear alerted us to danger, such as the presence of a saber-toothed tiger. Fear gave us a burst of adrenaline to enable us to run away or to fight. That physical reaction of elevated adrenaline was useful back then, but not any longer.

Fear does have a benefit, however. Think of fear like a yield sign when you are entering a highway. You don't need to stop—just slow down and pay attention to proceed safely. In the same way, when fear comes up, acknowledge it and pay attention to it. But don't let it stop you.

BE REALISTIC ABOUT RISK

A practical—and often overlooked—strategy for overcoming fear is to make sure you're not risking more than you can afford to lose.

To grow and achieve greater success, you have to risk something. Just make sure that you can handle the loss if you don't succeed the first time. My advice is to begin by taking on one challenge and then working your way up to more and bigger ones.

If you want to start your own business, but you need a guaranteed income each month to pay your mortgage and stay out of debt, you might want to start by running your business as a side hustle until you have enough clients to quit your day job for good.

If you're starting your first job in sales, you can work with an experienced person for a smaller commission as you learn the ropes. If you're eager to take on new responsibilities at work, start by asking to contribute to existing projects.

If you want to run a half marathon, start with a neighborhood 5K or 10K run.

Start taking action, move through your fears, learn new skills, and then take on more significant challenges.

FEAR IS LEARNED AND CAN BE UNLEARNED

There are only two fears that are built into your body at birth: the fear of loud noises and the fear of falling backward. Every other fear you have, you *learned*. Every one of them! That includes any fear of snakes, dogs, spiders, losing face, being embarrassed, talking to a large audience, or the fear of what others might think of you if you have more money than they have. The good news is that since you learned or created every fear you have, you can also *un*learn and un-create them.

HOW TO UNLEARN FEAR

The first step in "unlearning" fear is to realize that fear is the result of a visual image you have in your mind of an unpleasant future outcome. You may be familiar with the acronym **F.E.A.R.**—**F**antasized **E**xperience **A**ppearing **R**eal. When you realize that fear is the result of holding a negative image of an unwanted outcome in your head, you can do something about it. Here are a couple of options.

Option 1: Acknowledge the Fear

The first step in reducing fear is to become aware and to notice that fear is present. Stop for a moment. No, really—stop what you are doing, and notice the fear.

You can begin to put some distance between you and the fear by *"objectifying"* it. Instead of saying *I am afraid* to yourself, say *I am feeling fear*. Let's say you are starting a business and you want to ask someone to use your services. When you are preparing for the conversation and fear comes up, as it likely will the first few times, stop and recognize the fear and say, *I am feeling fear.* Then breathe.

Option 2: Feel the Fear

Another way to reduce fear is to allow yourself to actually *feel* the fear. This can be uncomfortable, and that is why many people will avoid this discomfort by instead putting off the needed action, or by eating or drinking too much in order to numb out the feeling, or they will get busy doing something other than what they need to do to distract themselves, or they will try to use humor to deflect it, as though it were not really important to them. Men especially don't like to admit they're afraid because it goes against their conditioning to not display softer, or what they interpret as weaker or more vulnerable, emotions.

You can choose to do what successful people do and allow yourself to feel the fear instead of running from it. You can practice this now by thinking of something you are afraid to do. And then simply feel the fear. You can use the following questions to bring your fear more into focus:

> *How strong is the fear, on a scale of 1 to 10?*
> *Where in my body does it feel the strongest? In my chest? In my abdomen? Around my shoulders or neck?*
> *Is it churning, or flowing, or is it stationary?*
> *If it had a color, what color would it be?*
> *If it had a shape, what shape would it be?*

You may find that by simply allowing yourself to feel these physical sensations, the fear will subside enough for you to take the needed action.

Option 3: Stop Imagining the Negative Outcome

Once you realize that you are creating the fear in your imagination, you can choose to stop it. Stop imagining the negative outcome you are creating in your mind. If this does not quell the fear enough for you to take the needed action, proceed to Option 4.

Option 4: Use Mindfulness to Stop Imagining the Negative Outcome

Another technique to reduce the fear is to bring your attention back to the present moment using mindfulness. (See *Chapter 12: Practice Meditation* for more information.) With mindfulness, you focus on your breath, and whenever your mind wanders, such as to the imagined negative outcome, you can bring your attention back to the present moment and breathe.

This process helps you to realize that nothing bad is really happening to you right now in the present moment. In order to create fear, you have to go into the future. When you stay in the present (by practicing mindfulness, for instance), you are fine. Even if someone had a gun pointed at you, in order to feel fear, you would have to picture yourself in the future and imagine they will pull the trigger.

Option 5: Replace the Scary Image with a New Image

Another option is to use your imagination for your own benefit instead of against yourself. How? By actively replacing the negative image you are imagining with its opposite, positive image. For example, instead of imagining that I will feel awkward and make a fool of myself if I accept your invitation to dinner, I can imagine going to your house for dinner, with you welcoming me and opening a nice bottle of wine, and then sharing a delicious meal and some great conversation. (You will have the chance to apply this technique in an exercise later in this chapter.)

Option 6: Use EFT, or "Tapping Therapy"

One of the most powerful tools for releasing fears ever developed is a technique called EFT—Emotional Freedom Technique—commonly known as *tapping therapy* because it involves tapping on nine acupressure points on the body as you focus on your fear. I use it and teach it in almost all of my workshops and trainings. It is easy to learn and easy to do. To read more about tapping, check out *Tapping Into Ultimate Success: How to Overcome Any Obstacle and Skyrocket Your Results*, which I coauthored with EFT expert Pamela Bruner. For a video demonstration of tapping, visit: JackCanfield.com/workbook -resources.

Or you can use your smartphone to scan this QR code:

Option 7: Process the Fear

Finally, you can *process away* the fear by going back in your memory to the earliest time when you felt a similar feeling, and then asking yourself the set of powerfully transformative questions that are listed below.

Recently I was asked to coach a man who was quite successful, but who did not have the level of financial success he wanted. While he had been earning around $350,000 annually for several years, he was not able to rise above this amount. I suspected he had some fear, perhaps based on experiences early in life. I asked him to think back to any significant events regarding money that he had experienced growing up. He reported that when he was 10, his father bought the family a new truck.

A boyhood friend said judgmentally, "It must be nice to have so much money!"

Ever since that incident, he's had a negative mind-set about having more money than other people. This unspoken, unrecognized fear had stopped him from the success he wanted. Once he saw this connection, the fear lost its grip on him, and he was able to bring his adult resourcefulness to let go of this fear and reach the higher income he desired.

To process a fear you recognize in yourself, ask yourself questions such as these:

> *Can you remember times in the past when you felt this fear?*
> *Can you remember the first time you felt this fear, perhaps as a child?*
> *What limiting decision did you make or limiting belief did you take on as a result of this experience?*
> *Now that you are an adult, do you see that you have more healthy and self-affirming choices for what to think or how to respond in this situation?*
> *What are some of the new choices you are now able to consider?*

WHEN FEAR BECOMES A SIGNAL OF
BEING ON THE RIGHT PATH

If your dreams don't scare you, they are too small.

RICHARD BRANSON
The Founder of Virgin Airlines and 400 Other Companies

Successful people learn to not resist—or fear—their fear. They often develop a close relationship with fear, since it has been their companion during periods of excitement and their greatest success.

Danielle Blum is a good example. She grew up knowing what was expected of her: get good grades, go to college, get a degree, and excel in a profession. She followed the rules up to a point—she was afraid not to. But once Danielle graduated from college, she was ready to take some risks. She longed to travel and to see what people in the rest of the world were like, beyond the American shores.

When she thought of delaying graduate school and traveling on her own to Spain, along with it came tremendous fear. People around her told her it was a bad idea, and that because she was a woman, she shouldn't travel by herself.

"I felt such fear! I know it was the fear of the unknown. I had moments of panic and of wondering what would happen to me. I was scared that I would be making a mistake. Yet, I heard that inner voice saying I should follow my instincts," Danielle told me.

That was when she considered taking the big step: to book a plane reservation and to head overseas, all by herself. She'd never done anything like that before. She recalls:

There was a moment when I was on the Internet, ready to book the plane ticket, and I hesitated. I knew this would be a life-changing move for me, against the wishes and advice of my parents and others, and I was so scared. I paused for a moment, then . . . I clicked 'Purchase!' At that moment I realized, oh my gosh, I totally just overcame my deepest fear! I dared to take the leap. That was my first moment of overcoming fear and realizing that I could trust myself and I would be okay.

Danielle chose a future of excitement and fulfillment over fear.

Eventually, Danielle did that over and over and over again in her travels, and she's been doing it ever since in her business. She chose to say yes, to move beyond her fear, and decided that, no matter what the fear, she was never going to give up on going after the future she wants.

The fear hasn't stopped, says Danielle, but now she sees fear as a signal that she is taking a big step, and it empowers her. Not only did she start her own business, she founded an organization called Global Heart Project that empowers women in developing countries with training and coaching—all because Danielle now sees fear as a signal that she's on the right path.

> *He who is not every day conquering some fear has not learned the secret of life.*
> RALPH WALDO EMERSON
> Famous American Philosopher

The following exercises will allow you to deconstruct any fears that may be in your way of taking the action needed to reach your goals.

I'm Afraid To . . .

For this first exercise, list six actions you need to take to reach your goal but which bring up fear when you think of doing them.

For example,

1. I'm afraid to *create a Web site to announce my new coaching business.*
2. I'm afraid to *commit and set a goal to reduce my unhealthy weight.*
3. I'm afraid to *write and post my first blog.*
4. I'm afraid to *tell my partner that I want to quit my job and find work that is more meaningful and fulfilling.*
5. I'm afraid to *ask my husband about how much money we have and where it goes.*
6. I'm afraid to *sign up for next year's half marathon.*

Now it's your turn: Write six things you are afraid or hesitant *to do* that are necessary for you to do in order to reach your goal.

1. I'm afraid to _____.

2. I'm afraid to _____.

3. I'm afraid to _____.

4. I'm afraid to _____.

5. I'm afraid to _____.

6. I'm afraid to _____.

I Scare Myself by Imagining Negative Outcomes

For each action you listed, restate it using the following format.

Example:

I want to *write and post my first blog*, and I scare myself by imagining *that people will read it and think it is not very good.*

Now it's your turn:

1. I want to _____, and

    I scare myself by imagining _____.

2. I want to _____, and

    I scare myself by imagining _____.

3. I want to _____, and

    I scare myself by imagining _____.

4. I want to _____, and

    I scare myself by imagining _____.

5. I want to _____, and

    I scare myself by imagining _____.

6. I want to _____, and

    I scare myself by imagining _____.

Replace Your Imaginary Negative Outcomes

Now that you are aware of how you use your imagination to scare yourself with images of negative outcomes, you can use your imagination to create mental images of the opposite positive outcomes you truly want.

Example:

I want to _write and post my first blog._
My opposite positive image of the desired outcome is _I receive enthusiastic comments from people, and they inquire about my coaching services._

Now it's your turn: In the spaces below, write a positive image of the outcome you want for each action you need to take.

1. I want to _____.

   My opposite, positive image of the desired outcome is _____

   _____.

2. I want to _____.

   My opposite, positive image of the desired outcome is _____

   _____.

3. I want to _____.

   My opposite, positive image of the desired outcome is _____

   _____.

4. I want to _____.

   My opposite, positive image of the desired outcome is _____

   _____.

5. I want to _____.

   My opposite, positive image of the desired outcome is _____

   _____.

6. I want to _____.

   My opposite, positive image of the desired outcome is _____

   _____.

From now on, instead of scaring yourself, you can stop, take a deep breath, and choose to create a mental image of the positive outcome you desire.

Losers visualize the penalties of failure. Winners visualize the rewards of success.

WILLIAM S. GILBERT
Successful English Playwright Who Wrote 75 Plays and Operettas

Remember How You Triumphed in the Face of Fear

You've overcome countless fears to become the person you are today, whether it was learning to ride a bike, driving a car, or kissing someone you liked for the first time. Taking risks and opening yourself to new experiences is often scary. But when you face your fears and take action anyway, you build confidence in your abilities. Take advantage of that history now with the exercise below by recalling times when you triumphed in the face of fear.

In this exercise, jot down five different times in your past when you faced doing something important to you that was scary, yet you took action anyway and things turned out well for you.

Example:
One activity that I feared doing, which I did, and it turned out well, is: *I wanted to become a public speaker, and the first few times I had a paid speaking gig, I was nervous and scared days ahead of time. But I did it anyway, and now I have become a world-class speaker.*

Now It's Your Turn

1. One activity that I feared doing, which I did, and it turned out well, is: _____

   _____

   _____.

2. One activity that I feared doing, which I did, and it turned out well, is: _____

   _____

   _____.

3. One activity that I feared doing, which I did, and it turned out well, is: _____

_____

_____.

4. One activity that I feared doing, which I did, and it turned out well, is: _____

_____

_____.

5. One activity that I feared doing, which I did, and it turned out well, is: _____

_____

_____.

Although the Breakthrough Goal you're facing now—and the way in which your fear is showing up—may be different from what you've experienced in the past, you already know how to overcome your fears. You can see you've spent a lifetime doing it! So I encourage you to follow this advice:

Do the thing you fear and the death of fear is certain.

RALPH WALDO EMERSON
Famous American Philosopher

Overcoming hesitancy based on fear is the best possible way to grow as a person and achieve more success in life. Every successful person I know has been willing to take a leap of faith even though they were afraid. They knew that if they didn't act, they would miss the opportunity.

In the superhero movie *Spider-Man: Into the Spider-Verse*, Miles Morales is an average teenager who's on the brink of becoming the new Spider-Man after being bitten by a radioactive spider. He turns to the older Spider-Man for advice because he is afraid of using his new powers, asking, "How do you know when you're ready?"

Spider-Man replies: "You don't. It's a leap of faith."

Barring situations of real danger or imminent physical harm, you, too, will need to take a leap of faith to meet your goals because, ultimately, the only way you'll get past being afraid to do something is *to actually do it.* You'll feel more confident and more certain when you take the next risk.

You gain strength, courage, and confidence by every experience in which you really stop to look fear in the face . . . You must do the thing you think you cannot do.

ELEANOR ROOSEVELT
Former First Lady of the United States

DECIDE TO TAKE BOLD ACTION TODAY

What's the most valuable action you can take right now to get closer to achieving your goals? Take a moment to decide what it is, then commit to a time when you will take that step.

The bold action I will take is: _____

_____.

I will complete it by this date: _____.

Now, put this action item on your calendar and go to sleep tonight knowing you are on your way, further along toward the success you want.

Add to Your Life Success Journal

Turn to page 229 of *Your Life Success Journal* and complete the exercise for this chapter.

CHAPTER

9

ASK WITHOUT FEAR OF REJECTION*

The greatest gift is not being afraid to question.

RUBY DEE
American Actress, Playwright, Screenwriter, and Civil Rights Activist

Why do we stop ourselves from asking for assistance, asking for a date, asking for critical information, asking for the sale, asking for a raise, asking for a loan, asking for a discount, asking for an upgrade, asking for advice, or asking for anything else that we know would get us to our goal more easily and more quickly?

The answer is that most people are uncomfortable asking for what they want. How about you? Do you hesitate to boldly and directly ask for what you want? Or do you fear the pain and embarrassment of being rejected, looking foolish, admitting that you don't know something or that you need help? Do you feel you always have to look like you already know the answer, that you have it all together, that you can do it all by yourself, or that as the leader you have to project an image of always knowing what you are doing and being in control?

Can you think of three times in the last week when you went out of your comfort zone and asked someone for assistance, advice, or support? If not, you know what I am talking about.

Let's look more deeply at some of the reasons you might not be asking.

YOU DON'T KNOW THAT HELP IS AVAILABLE

As an individual, you can't possibly know all that is available about current technology, useful procedures, needed skills, helpful resources—or other details about

---

*Read *Principle 17: Ask! Ask! Ask!* in the book *The Success Principles* for more explanation, stories, and examples.

who or what is available to help you reach your goals. But the fact is that someone, somewhere, is likely to have the answer or solution you're looking for and could help you get what you need. That someone could make your life easier and reduce the hurdles you're facing—but you can only access these people and resources by asking those people for what you need.

YOU DEFER TO OTHERS WHO ARE SMARTER, WEALTHIER, OR MORE "SUCCESSFUL"

Another barrier to asking for what you need from those who may have the answer or the resources is that you defer to, or even avoid, those who seem to be smarter, more successful, better connected, older, or more powerful. Yet these people often have the knowledge you want and the wisdom you need because they have already achieved what you want to achieve. Contrary to popular belief, most successful people are often very willing to share their knowledge and advice with you. So don't let your fear of rejection prevent you from asking for assistance.

YOU DON'T REALLY KNOW WHAT YOU WANT OR NEED

I'm tough, I'm ambitious, and I know exactly what I want.

MADONNA
Singer, Songwriter, Actress, and Winner of Eight Grammys

Perhaps the biggest reason most people fail to ask for what they need is that they aren't exactly sure about what they want or need. One of the reasons I asked you to clearly define what you want in *Chapter 3: Decide What You Want* is that asking (for anything) becomes much easier when you're clear, specific, focused, and confident in your request.

Having clarity gives you confidence, while a lack of self-assurance—which results in asking for help in a timid, vague, and awkward way—won't get you very far. Much of the time, other people want to help and will respond to reasonable requests, but you've got to meet them halfway by clearly stating your goal, correctly defining your problem or your need, and carefully stating the solution or the help you're seeking.

THE MOST OBVIOUS NEXT STEP

Remember the eight categories of your life from *Chapter 3: Decide What You Want*? Let's stop for a moment and think about what things you would need to ask for to achieve success in each of them. You might ask for something outright like a car or a free vacation rental (and get it)—or you might have to ask for the information, resources, guidance, or assistance that will help you eventually accomplish your goal(s).

Well, if you could ask for just one thing that would get you started with achieving your biggest goal in each of the seven areas, what would that one thing be? I recommend that you determine the *next most obvious step you could take in achieving that goal* and ask someone for something that would help with that.

The Most Obvious Next Step: What Will You Ask For?

In the exercise below, choose your most heartfelt or meaningful desire or need in each of the seven areas, then answer the questions that follow.

My Finances

My most important want or need is _____

_____.

The next most obvious step to achieving what I want or need is _____

_____.

Who can I ask for help? _____

What will I ask for? _____

My Work, Career, or Business

My most important want or need is _____

_____.

The next most obvious step to achieving what I want or need is _____

_____.

Who can I ask for help? _____

What will I ask for? _____

My Relationships

My most important want or need is _____

_____.

The next most obvious step to achieving what I want or need is _____

_____.

Who can I ask for help? _____

What will I ask for? _____

My Health and Fitness

My most important want or need is _____

_____.

The next most obvious step to achieving what I want or need is _____

_____.

Who can I ask for help? _____

What will I ask for? _____

My Free Time, Fun, and Recreation

My most important want or need is _____

_____.

The next most obvious step to achieving what I want or need is _____

_____.

Who can I ask for help? _____

What will I ask for? _____

My Personal and Spiritual Growth

My most important want or need is _____

_____.

The next most obvious step to achieving what I want or need is _____

_____.

Who can I ask for help? _____

What will I ask for? _____

My Possessions
My most important want or need is _____

_____.

The next most obvious step to achieving what I want or need is _____

_____.

Who can I ask for help? _____

What will I ask for? _____

Making a Difference and Being of Service
My most important want or need is _____

_____.

The next most obvious step to achieving what I want or need is _____

_____.

Who can I ask for help? _____

What will I ask for? _____

ASK IN SPITE OF THE FEAR OF REJECTION

Even when we *do* know the next steps—even when we *do* know what to ask for—far too often we still don't ask because we want to avoid looking foolish, being vulnerable, losing face, or triggering memories of negative episodes in the past where we asked and were soundly rejected or humiliated.

But what if you faced your fear of rejection? What if you could learn to ask *regardless of* your fear of rejection?

ASK WITHOUT THE FEAR OF REJECTION

Tony Robbins tells the story of being in New York City one year and deciding to deliver some meals to the homeless. He sent his team to rent a van, and they came back empty-handed. They said no vans were available; because of the Thanksgiving holidays, they had all been rented. Tony decided to use the power of *asking without fear of rejection*. He would go himself and ask for a van. But who would he ask? Well, he stopped every person who was driving a van down the street in front of his hotel and asked if they would let him use their van.

In spite of many rejections, Tony was not to be deterred. As yet another van approached, he once again flagged down the driver. It turned out that this driver was the director of the Salvation Army for all of New York and was in the business of delivering food to the needy. Tony purchased baskets of food for nearly 40 people, loaded the van, and together they delivered the food to a group of the homeless in a burned-out building in the South Bronx.

IS THE FEAR OF REJECTION STOPPING YOU?

It's possible that the fear of someone rejecting you may be stopping you. But let's look at what's really happening when you fail to ask: *You are the one who is rejecting yourself in advance of ever asking.* You're the one saying no to yourself before anyone else has a chance to.

And the saddest part is the person you ask might say *yes!*

Don't assume that someone will decline your request. (Even if they do, you're no worse off than you were before asking. You are in the same place before you asked. It didn't get worse!) Plus, there's almost always a benefit to asking—even when they say no. You might learn something you didn't know before, you might find out about a better person to ask, you'll likely create some new connections, you'll get better at presenting your request, and you'll probably discover how to work your way through the system better—or you'll gain more confidence in yourself and a more deep-seated conviction for attaining your goal.

FEAR OF REJECTION: THE COST OF NOT ASKING

For each need or want you identified above, determine what keeps you from asking. Answering the questions about each category below will not only help you discover where your fears come from—it will help you move past your fears to the more significant benefits awaiting you.

EXAMPLE: My Finances

What do I need to ask for? *I need to ask my business partner to repay the money I lent to him.*

How do I stop myself from asking? *I scare myself by imagining he will get angry, say I don't trust him, and cause a rift in our business.*

What is it costing me not to ask? *It is costing me $2,000, plus my wife is angry that we cannot afford some of the things she wants to buy and do.*

What benefit(s) would I get if I asked? *I would stop worrying and obsessing about it. I would have more discretionary money to spend, and my wife would get off my back about it.*

My Finances

What do I need to ask for? _____

_____

How do I stop myself from asking? _____

_____

What is it costing me not to ask? _____

What benefit(s) would I get if I asked? _____

_____

My Work, Career, or Business

What do I need to ask for? _____

_____

How do I stop myself from asking? _____

_____

What is it costing me not to ask? _____

What benefit(s) would I get if I asked? _____

_____

My Relationships

What do I need to ask for? _____

_____

How do I stop myself from asking? _____

_____

What is it costing me not to ask? _____

What benefit(s) would I get if I asked? _____

_____

My Health and Fitness

What do I need to ask for? _____

_____

How do I stop myself from asking? _____

_____

What is it costing me not to ask? _____

What benefit(s) would I get if I asked? _____

_____

My Free Time, Fun, and Recreation

What do I need to ask for? _____

_____

How do I stop myself from asking? _____

_____

What is it costing me not to ask? _____

What benefit(s) would I get if I asked? _____

_____

My Personal and Spiritual Growth

What do I need to ask for? _____

_____

How do I stop myself from asking? _____

_____

What is it costing me not to ask? _____

What benefit(s) would I get if I asked? _____

_____

My Possessions
What do I need to ask for? _____

_____.

How do I stop myself from asking? _____

_____.

What is it costing me not to ask? _____

What benefit(s) would I get if I asked? _____

Making a Difference and Being of Service
What do I need to ask for? _____

_____

How do I stop myself from asking? _____

_____

What is it costing me not to ask? _____

What benefit(s) would I get if I asked? _____

_____

HOW TO ASK FOR WHAT YOU WANT

If you went through your day without the fear of rejection, your entire life would change. You would know how, when, and whom to ask for anything you want to know, accomplish, or acquire. You'd experience fewer disappointments because you would be making better decisions from a place of having more and better information, instead of being disadvantaged by your lack of experience. You would have better relationships because you would have done the difficult work of having made your requests known instead of silently resenting the other person for not reading your mind and giving you what you want and feel you deserve. You would get more of the support you need in all areas of your life (because you asked for it), instead of suffering from despair and loneliness. So many aspects of your life will improve once you begin asking.

Here's a formula you can use to improve your chances of getting a yes.★

Ask As If You Expect to Get It

You can set up a positive expectation in your mind when you ask as if you expect to get what you're asking for. In turn, this expectation adds power to your request because it affects everything else—your body posture, your eye contact, your tone of voice, and even your choice of words.

You've probably heard the difference between someone who is asking timidly versus someone who is asking with the expectation of succeeding. The timid person ends their question with a little inflection or lilt in their voice, while the confident person states the question firmly—as if they are just placing an order for an item they want and expect to get.

Here are some phrases that convey confidence and positive expectation. *I'd like to get . . . I'd like to inquire whether . . . My research tells me that you're the one who can . . .* All of these convey more confidence than *I was wondering if you could possibly . . . ? I hate to bother you, but would you be willing to . . . ?*

Ask Someone Who Can Give It to You

Not everyone can deliver on your request. Even fewer people can "plus it" into something even better than you expected. Your job is to research and assess whether or not you're asking the right person.

For example, if you're looking for someone to be a partner in a new venture, ask if they're even in a position to invest their time and money on a new project

---

★If you would like to learn even more about how to ask for what you want and get it, read *The Aladdin Factor* by Jack Canfield and Mark Victor Hansen (available from Amazon.com and Barnes&Noble .com) or listen to the audio version of the book. We also developed a six-hour audio course by the same name—*The Aladdin Factor: How to Ask for and Get Anything You Want*—that is available at JackCanfield .com.

before you spend an hour sharing your plans with them. If you're asking someone to mentor you in your career—that is, helping you make good decisions and avoid bad ones—make sure they have the career experience and emotional maturity to advise you.

Be Clear and Specific When You Ask

If you want more money, be clear and specific about *how much* money when you ask your boss for a raise, ask an investor for funding, or ask a new customer to purchase your services.

If you're asking a bank for a loan, be clear and specific about how much money you need to expand your business. If you're asking your teenager for more help around the house or asking your spouse for more time with them, be specific about exactly what you want them to do.

> **NOT USEFUL:** I want more help around the house.
> **USEFUL:** I'd like you to do the dishes and take out the trash every night after dinner.
> **NOT USEFUL:** I want to spend more time with you.
> **USEFUL:** I want you home for dinner at least four nights a week, and I want to plan six long weekends a year to go someplace fun.

Ask for What You Want, Not for What You Don't Want

Psychologists know that the brain has difficulty registering negative words like *don't, can't, not,* and *never.* So when you ask for anything, put it in a positive statement of what you *do want*, instead of stating what you don't want.

> **NOT EFFECTIVE:** I want you to not yell at me anymore.
> **EFFECTIVE:** When you're upset, I want you to speak to me in a normal tone of voice. If you feel yourself losing your

cool, I want you to stop and take a time-out to calm down.

NOT EFFECTIVE: I don't want to have to give the reports back to you because of errors.

EFFECTIVE: Before bringing me the reports, I want you to check them against last month's numbers, and then cross-check the amounts with this month's P&L from Accounting.

Ask Repeatedly

Children know this rule well. They ask for what they want over and over again until somebody says yes. Why not do the same as adults? When someone says, *NO!*, your response should be, *NEXT!*

Next can refer to asking the next person on your list of people or to asking the same person you just asked at some later date.

Of course, it's easier to adopt this mind-set when you realize that a *No* doesn't mean "Stop!" It may mean *not yet, not now, you've called the wrong department, I'm not authorized to do that, you haven't met the proper criteria yet*, or any number of other possibilities. When you keep asking the same or different people, you can gain new information, learn how to ask more effectively, discover who the right people are, and learn to ask with greater clarity and greater confidence.

WHAT'S THE BEST THING THAT COULD HAPPEN?

Sometimes you will be surprised when you receive even more than you asked for. In the next exercise, I'm going to ask you to stretch your thinking and imagine the *best possible outcome* you could get from asking. Too often, we expect a no, and so we never ask in the first place. Psychologist Dr. Nathaniel Branden developed a technique that helps you retrain your mind to expect a more positive outcome by using the technique of rapid-fire sentence completion to bypass your usual habitual patterns of negative thinking.

IMAGINING THE BEST POSSIBLE OUTCOMES

In the following exercise, write down five to ten endings for each of the following incomplete sentences. Do it as rapidly as you can, without stopping to think about what you're writing. Don't worry about whether your answers are possible, reasonable, or "allowed." Just write down your answers as fast as you can.

1. If I could get what I wanted, my life would be . . .

_____

_____

_____

_____

_____

2. If the person I was asking could fulfill my request, they would . . .

_____

_____

_____

_____

_____

3. I can expand my thinking by dreaming of getting what I ask for, plus . . .

_____

_____

_____

_____

_____

4. If my request were honored, my next steps after that would be . . .

_____

_____

_____

_____

_____

5. If they went beyond my request and delivered even more than I asked for, they would . . .

_____

_____

_____

_____

_____

MAKE-IT-A-HABIT WORKSHEET
Plan Your "Asks" Each Day

Here's an exercise you can use each day that will help you to build the new habit of asking—with confidence. As you jot down your Rule of 5 tasks for the day, put a check mark beside those tasks where you'll have to ask for something needed to reach your goal.

Answer the following questions:

1. What do I need to ask for? _____

2. Who do I need to ask? _____

3. What, specifically, do I want to receive? _____

4. If there were anything that would stop me from asking (internally or externally), what would that be?

_____

5. What's the cost of not asking? _____

6. What's the possible benefit of asking? _____

7. What talking points do I need to keep in mind? _____

_____

_____

Add to Your Life Success Journal

Turn to page 230 of *Your Life Success Journal* and complete the exercise for this chapter.

CHAPTER

10

ASK FOR FEEDBACK EARLY AND OFTEN*

*We all need people who will give us feedback.
That's how we improve.*

BILL GATES
The Founder of Microsoft and Whose Net Worth Is $110 Billion

No one knows the perfect path to their goals. It remains to be discovered, trying one thing then another. When you're going after something new, like your Breakthrough Goal, you start by taking the smartest action you know. After that, you seek feedback to determine what is working well and what is not. You can work toward achieving your goals more easily and quickly with feedback. That is what successful people do. They learn to solicit, welcome, gracefully receive, consider, and then act on whatever feedback is available to them.

You are always in charge of whom to ask for feedback, how to ask for feedback, when to ask for feedback, and how to respond to the feedback you receive in the most effective way. A valuable time to ask for feedback is when things are not going as well as you'd like. You can ask others for their input on how to correct the situation. You will begin to see that mistakes and challenges are merely opportunities to learn, grow, and change—and to do better in the future.

And when things are going well? You can ask others for feedback on how you can maintain it and improve things even more.

---

*Read *Principle 19: Use Feedback to Your Advantage* in the book *The Success Principles* for more explanation, stories, and examples.

POSITIVE AND NEGATIVE FEEDBACK

Once you begin to take action, you'll start getting feedback on how you are doing. Some feedback will be positive, and some negative. Of course, we all prefer positive feedback—we love to hear what we are doing well. When you ask others for feedback, the feedback you receive may be perceived as negative because people often tend to focus on what's missing or less-than-perfect about what we're doing. That's why it's the exceptional teacher, parent, or boss who focuses on the positive—that is, praise, encouragement, results, money, promotions, satisfied customers, awards, happiness, inner peace, intimacy, or pleasure.

> *There are two things people want more than sex and money: recognition and praise.*
>
> MARY KAY ASH
> The Founder of Mary Kay Cosmetics

We tend not to like negative feedback, which can take the form of lack of results, little or no money, criticism, poor evaluations, being passed over for a raise or promotion, complaints, unhappiness, inner conflict, loneliness, and emotional and physical pain.

However, negative feedback provides valuable information. One of the most useful things you can do is change how you respond to "negative" feedback. Begin to think of it as corrective feedback that simply tells you that you are "off course" on your path to success. Think of it as simply an opportunity for improvement.

BECOME DISPASSIONATELY NEUTRAL TO FEEDBACK

Because you're likely to receive more negative feedback than positive feedback when you're first learning how to do something, you need to become dispassionately neutral to it. When you can remain neutral, you will avoid the three ways that don't work when responding to feedback.

First: Don't Cave In or Quit

Negative feedback does not mean you are stupid, incompetent, or incapable of achieving your goals. Negative feedback is not a stop sign or a death sentence. Unfortunately, too many people cave in or quit when they receive negative or critical feedback. Your #1 priority is to continue to pursue your goals until you reach them.

Successful people keep their eye on the prize and learn to accept feedback gracefully. They recognize that occasional poor results are part of the process. They look to find the lesson in the feedback, and they keep on keeping on. When you receive negative feedback, learn from it, course-correct, and plot a new path toward your goal. Remember, the feedback is not about you as a human being—it is information about a specific action, behavior, or way of being. There is a useful acronym to keep in mind: QTIP—Quit Taking It Personally!

Second: Don't Get Mad at the Messenger

The second response to negative feedback that doesn't work is to get mad at the person giving you the feedback. Yes, feedback can hurt, and your first reaction may be anger. Just take a breath and let it go. You want to encourage feedback, even negative feedback—and even when it stings. The best possible response to feedback is to say (and to mean it), "Thank you for caring enough to give me this feedback." Any feedback gives you information you can use to better meet your goal.

Third: Don't Ignore It

The third response to negative feedback that doesn't work is to ignore it or to dismiss it out of hand. You may know someone who does this—they tune out everyone else's point of view. We call these people "feedback proof." No matter what others say, they think they are always right, and they do things their way, even when it is not working. They not only don't benefit from other people's good ideas, but their relationships often suffer as well.

Because you want to reach a higher level of success and achieve a Breakthrough Goal that is a stretch for you, you need to be a learning machine, taking in all the positive and negative feedback you can gather. In the advanced trainings

I conduct several times a year, the participants get to know one another pretty well. Toward the end of the week, I have them mill about and ask each other, "How do you see me limiting myself?" After 30 minutes, the participants sit down and make notes about what they learned—looking for patterns. Some of the comments may seem irrelevant or off target. These they put aside. For the other comments, they process this information and develop an action plan for addressing these limitations. When you are focused on growing and reaching important goals, you welcome and value the feedback. By the way, the participants typically evaluate this as one of the most beneficial exercises in the seminar. How do I know this? Because, like every successful seminar leader, I also ask for feedback at the end of each seminar. I'm never offended by any of the feedback, and I use what the participants say to make the next seminar better. I take to heart what leadership author Ken Blanchard says: "Feedback is the breakfast of champions."

A BALANCE OF NEGATIVE AND POSITIVE FEEDBACK

Which type of feedback do you prefer, negative or positive? Most people say positive, of course. It makes you feel good. It confirms what you are doing right. But can you remember times in your life when negative feedback was useful?

Negative feedback, although sometimes painful, is the information you need to seek out when you are off track. Successful people often report that their most significant growth has come from the negative feedback they received as a result of a failure at work, or from a problematic relationship in their personal lives. The truth is, both negative and positive feedback are needed. It is like the two poles on a battery—both are required to produce electricity.

IS ALL FEEDBACK ACCURATE?

When your two-year-old son tells you your soufflé doesn't taste good, it's not likely to be all that accurate—or useful. He may simply be too young to have developed a sophisticated palate. Likewise, an adult who gives you feedback may have a distorted view of you because of something random such as you look like their uncle who teased them without end when they were four years old. A good idea is for you to get feedback from multiple people so that you can look for a pattern. Once you hear from several people that you're either overbearing or too quiet in meetings, it is time to consider it.

If one person tells you you're a horse, they're crazy. If three people tell you you're a horse, there's a conspiracy afoot. If ten people tell you you're a horse, it's time to buy a saddle.

JACK ROSENBLUM
Corporate Consultant

MAKING IT SAFE FOR FEEDBACK

When you are soliciting feedback, you want to remember to keep things safe: protection for the person offering the feedback and safety for you as the receiver. Let's talk about you first. If you think the person you're asking for feedback might be harsh with you, you can set the tone in advance by stating that you're asking because you want to improve, and that you trust they'll present their feedback in a way that will contribute and benefit you. Of course, between the lines, you're actually saying, "Please give me helpful information—not just that you think I'm a jerk." You can also ask that they treat your request respectfully and with empathy.

Criticism, like rain, should be gentle enough to nourish a man's growth without destroying his roots.

FRANK A. CLARK

If someone has been especially critical of you, remember that for them to see where you're limiting yourself, they have to know that you have more potential than you are currently showing. They may tell you that they see you selling yourself short, or that you're not asking for enough money, that you're getting angry all the time, or something else. Take it as corrective feedback and not as a judgment about you. Focus on the parts that are helpful to you.

To make it safe for the people you're asking for feedback, it's a good idea to assure them of your intentions and to offer them safety. Some people might be taken aback by your request, so you're likely to get more honest and direct feedback if you tell them, "I really want to hear what you have to say." You can add,

"I promise not to be offended by what you say. I'm interested in my personal and professional growth, and I want to be a better person [friend, spouse, entrepreneur, employee, supervisor]. Your feedback can help me to be more successful."

Asking for Feedback in Your Business Life

Think of one or more of the work-related goals you are pursuing. With that in mind, answer the questions below to develop a plan for gathering feedback that will assist you in reaching your biggest goal.

What Feedback Do I Need to Ask for That I'm Not Asking for Now?	Who Should I Ask? How Many People Should I Ask?	When Will I Ask?	How Will I Ask?
Example: *Is my new service appealing? What do you like about it? What fee should I charge? How do I add more value? Might other groups be interested in purchasing it?*	*Customers; clients; experts; vendors; other practitioners. At least 30 people.*	*By June 30th. Ask at each Meet-Up, networking event, and group presentation.*	*Face-to-face, phone calls, a question to the group.*
Source #1			
Source #2			
Source #3			
Source #4			

Asking for Feedback in Personal Relationships

Personal relationships are the most important relationships in our lives. Use your new skills and your awareness of the value of feedback to gather input from those you care about most.

Ask for feedback from at least three family members, close friends, your romantic partner, mentors, or others using the questions below.

Person #1

1. On a scale of 1 to 10, how would you rate the quality of our relationship over this past week/month/year?

_____

2. What positive things did I do to get that rating? (Why so high?)

_____

_____

3. If you gave me a rating of anything less than a 10, what would it take to make it a 10?

_____

_____

Person #2

1. On a scale of 1 to 10, how would you rate the quality of our relationship over this past week/month/year?

_____

2. What positive things did I do to get that rating? (Why so high?)

_____

_____

3. If you gave me a rating of anything less than a 10, what would it take to make it a 10?

_____

_____

Person #3

1. On a scale of 1 to 10, how would you rate the quality of our relationship over this past week/month/year?

_____

2. What positive things did I do to get that rating? (Why so high?)

_____

_____

3. If you gave me a rating of anything less than a 10, what would it take to make it a 10?

_____

_____

Asking for Feedback About Your Future Success

Here are two terrific questions to ask a colleague.

Question #1 solicits negative feedback: _How do you see me limiting myself?_

Question #2 solicits positive feedback: _How do you see me contributing to my success?_

Ask someone who knows you, knows what you are up to, and is aware of the goals you have set for yourself.

1. **First person:** Whom will you ask? _____

   When will you ask her or him? _____

2. **Second person:** Whom will you ask? _____

   When will you ask her or him? _____

3. **Third person:** Whom will you ask? _____

   When will you ask her or him? _____

Action Plan Based on Your Feedback

Now that you have obtained feedback from several sources, answer the questions below to consolidate what you have learned and to make a plan for your continued success.

What are the major points that you heard?

_____

_____

_____

What are your thoughts about what you heard? How do you feel about the feedback?

_____

_____

_____

What actions will you take based on the feedback you received? (Notice that this is the point of asking for feedback: to learn from it and then to do something different in the future as a result.)

_____

_____

_____

MAKE-IT-A-HABIT WORKSHEET
Make Time to Solicit Feedback

Take out your calendar and schedule a time this week to complete the exercises in this chapter. Make sure to do this now, before moving on.

Add to Your Life Success Journal

Turn to page 230 of *Your Life Success Journal* and complete the exercise for this chapter.

CHAPTER

11

PRACTICE PERSISTENCE*

It's always too soon to quit.

NORMAN VINCENT PEALE
Author of *The Power of Positive Thinking*

If there's one quality that differentiates successful people more than anything else, it's that they persist. They keep working toward their goal no matter what. They never quit. When faced with obstacles, they keep going, they keep trying new things, and they keep at it—until they reach their final goal.

The Google Dictionary defined *persistence* as "firm or obstinate continuance in a course of action in spite of difficulty or opposition."

Practicing persistence means that you have to continue taking action toward your goal despite the challenges, difficulties, setbacks, or temporary failures you encounter along the way.

And the fact is, you will almost always face challenges.

They are part of the process of achieving anything worthwhile. Companies lose customers and market share, entrepreneurs run out of money, athletes get injured, manuscripts get rejected, actors don't get the part they want, salespeople get turned down, checks bounce, equipment breaks down, necessary parts don't arrive on time, and people you trust don't keep their commitments. There will be times when you may feel discouraged, and you may even be tempted to quit. But to make sure you persevere and don't quit, here are three things you can do to be prepared for those times when you feel like giving up.

1. Acknowledge and accept that having to deal with challenges, difficulties, setbacks, and failures is a natural part of the process.

---

*Read *Principle 22: Practice Persistence* in the book *The Success Principles* for more explanation, stories, and examples.

2. Be ready and willing to respond to any challenges that arise and make any necessary corrections based on the feedback you receive.

3. Be prepared with a Plan B. Take time before you begin to think of all the obstacles that you might face, all the things that could go wrong, and all the challenges that could come up—then formulate a plan for how you will respond to each one, if they should occur.

If achieving everything you wanted were easy, you would already have everything you want. The truth is that when you pursue a goal that you've never achieved before, there's a learning curve you must go through, and that usually means you're going to have to step outside your comfort zone and do things you've never done before. Whether your Breakthrough Goal is to become wealthy, to reach your ideal weight, to start your own company, to renew your relationship with your spouse, to win a major award, or to break a world record, you need to acknowledge that it will take *time* and *effort*, as well as require you to do new things that you're *uncomfortable* doing.

By applying the success principles you're learning in this *Workbook* as you're pursuing your goals, you'll be making it as easy as possible to succeed. Despite that, however, you can expect obstacles and challenges along the way. It's just the normal course of pursuing something new. These challenges may include *external roadblocks*—such as a lack of funding for your project, opposition from your partner or your parents, or difficulty finding competent employees. Or they might be *internal obstacles* such as a lack of experience, self-doubt, and fear.

Even when some part of you wants to say, "I quit!" you'll need to continue in order to reach your goal. Here are some strategies that will help you persevere.

REWARD YOURSELF ALONG THE WAY

Break your larger goal into smaller milestones that need to be achieved, and reward yourself when you accomplish these subgoals. Take your spouse or a friend out for a special dinner, treat yourself to a massage, or take a day off to do something fun.

TO PERSIST, SEEK INSPIRATION

One way to keep yourself motivated to persist through the hard times is to surround yourself with inspirational quotes like these. (You can also find hundreds more on the Internet by searching "quotes on perseverance and persistence.")

When you're going through hell, keep moving.

Attributed to WINSTON CHURCHILL
Former Prime Minister of Great Britain

Energy and persistence conquer all things.

BENJAMIN FRANKLIN
One of the Founding Fathers of the United States of America

Nothing in this world can take the place of persistence. Talent will not; nothing is more common than unsuccessful men with talent. Genius will not; unrewarded genius is almost a proverb. Education will not; the world is full of educated derelicts. Persistence and determination alone are omnipotent.

Attributed to CALVIN COOLIDGE
30th President of the United States of America

Ambition is the path to success. Persistence is the vehicle you arrive in.

BILL BRADLEY
Member of the NBA Hall of Fame

Champions keep playing until they get it right.

BILLIE JEAN KING
Former World #1 Professional Tennis Player

If you can't fly then run, if you can't run then walk, if you can't walk then crawl, but whatever you do you have to keep moving forward.

DR. MARTIN LUTHER KING, JR.
American Civil Rights Leader

*Making your mark on the world is hard. If it were easy, everybody would
do it. But it's not. It takes patience, it takes commitment, and it comes with
plenty of failures along the way. The real test is not whether you avoid this
failure, because you won't. It's whether you let it harden or shame you into
inaction, or whether you learn from it; whether you choose to persevere.*

BARACK OBAMA
44th President of the United States of America

Perseverance is falling 19 times and succeeding the 20th.

JULIE ANDREWS
Academy Award-Winning Actress

*The lesson that I have learned and follow all my life is that we
should try and try and try again—but never give up!*

RICHARD BRANSON
Founder of Virgin Airlines

It doesn't matter how slowly you go as long as you do not stop.

CONFUCIUS
Chinese Philosopher and Politician

Money grows on the tree of persistence.

JAPANESE PROVERB

READ INSPIRATIONAL BIOGRAPHIES, AUTOBIOGRAPHIES, AND STORIES

Another way to keep yourself motivated to persevere in the face of obstacles is to
read the stories of people who have achieved great things by persevering against
all odds. Here are some of my favorite books:

- *Shark Tales: How I Turned $1,000 into a Billion Dollar Business* by Barbara Corcoran
- *Born Standing Up: A Comic's Life* by Steve Martin
- *I Am Malala: The Girl Who Stood Up for Education and Was Shot by the Taliban* by Malala Yousafzai
- *The Pursuit of Happyness* by Chris Gardner

- *Long Walk to Freedom* by Nelson Mandela
- *Wild: From Lost to Found on the Pacific Crest Trail* by Cheryl Strayed

One biographical story about perseverance that inspires me is the story of long-distance swimmer Diana Nyad.

Growing up in New York City, a place that doesn't usually come to mind when one thinks of the birthplace of great swimmers, Diana had parents who were always able to find a pool for her. She especially loved swimming long distances. She just kept swimming and swimming, doing what she loved. When Diana was 26, she shocked everyone by swimming around the island of Manhattan—28 miles without stopping. She became famous for her endurance swims. And then she set an even bigger goal: to swim from Havana, Cuba, to Key West, Florida—an astonishing 112 miles.

To get ready, she trained by doing 12-hour workouts of nonstop swimming, then 14-, 18-, 20-, and eventually 24-hour workouts. Imagine! She would swim for 24 hours straight!

Sports physiology studies have shown that in such marathon-type activities, one's mental determination is a more critical factor than the physical energy and capabilities. From 1978 to 2012, Diana tried four times to make it from Cuba to Florida. Each time she "failed."

When she was 64 years old (64!), she tried one more time to make the swim, all the way from Cuba to Key West. Finally, after 53 hours straight, fighting currents and jellyfish, she made it—112 statute miles, nonstop, setting a record.

Here, in her own words, is her advice to anyone pursuing a dream:

> Find a way. Find your grit. There's a place in you that you have gone before. It's the source of your strength, and it's the source that you called upon each time you accomplished something important to you. That is your greatest asset. That is the place you need to draw upon again. As you think about what is most important to you, that is the resource you'll draw upon to make the new thing happen. It's about finding your grit and your will. Find a way.

LISTEN TO MUSIC AND SONGS THAT UPLIFT AND INSPIRE YOU

Create a playlist of music, songs, and power anthems with music and lyrics that motivate you and pump you up. Play the songs on that playlist when you first get up in the morning, while you're running or working out, and whenever you're feeling like you need a boost to keep going. Here are a few suggestions:

- "Chariots of Fire" by Vangelis (instrumental)
- "Roar" by Katy Perry
- "The Champion" by Carrie Underwood (featuring Ludacris)
- "One Step at a Time" by Jordan Sparks
- "We Are the Champions" by Queen
- "Larger Than Life" by Backstreet Boys
- "Brave Faith" and "If I Were Brave" by Jana Stanfield
- "You Gotta Want It" by Roberta Gold
- "Get on Your Feet" by Gloria Estefan
- "Fame" by Irene Cara
- "When You Believe" by Mariah Carey and Whitney Houston
- "You Will Win" by Jekalyn Carr (Christian-themed lyrics)
- "Born to Fly" by Sara Evans
- "I'm Gonna Be Somebody" by Travis Tritt

WATCH INSPIRATIONAL AND MOTIVATIONAL MOVIES

Another great way to stay motivated and persevere when times are tough is to watch inspirational movies like

127 Hours	*How We Made Our Millions*	*Soul Surfer*
42		*Slumdog Millionaire*
A Beautiful Mind	*Invincible*	*The Blind Side*
Billy Elliot	*Joy*	*The Rookie*
Cinderella Man	*Miracle*	*Unbreakable*
Cool Running	*Moneyball*	*We Are Marshall*
Gandhi	*Radio*	*The Hundred-Foot Journey*
Hoop Dreams	*Rocky*	*The Shawshank Redemption*
Hoosiers	*Remember the Titans*	*The Theory of Everything*
Hotel Rwanda	*Rudy*	*The Pursuit of Happyness*
Invictus	*Seabiscuit*	

You can watch trailers of all these movies on the Internet to see which ones appeal to you the most.

CONSIDER THIS

- Oprah Winfrey was fired from her first two television jobs.
- Academy Award–winner Steven Spielberg applied to the University of Southern California School of Cinema-Television, three times—and was rejected three times. He eventually went to California State University, Long Beach, where he later dropped out and decided to pursue a directing career without a degree.
- When Howard Schultz, the founder of Starbucks, was raising the money to open the first three stores, he talked to 242 banks and investors, and 217 said no before he raised the necessary funding needed to proceed.
- Henry Ford went bankrupt five times before he finally succeeded with the Ford Motor Company.
- Before Harlan Sanders became famous as Colonel Sanders, he tried to sell his fried chicken recipe to 1,009 restaurants before finding a buyer.
- Thomas Edison "failed" more than 1,000 times before he successfully invented the electric lightbulb.
- Walt Disney was fired by a newspaper editor for lack of ideas. He then went bankrupt several times before he built Disneyland and eventually launched one of the most beloved brands in history.
- Theodore Geisel, better known as Dr. Seuss, had his first book *And to Think That I Saw It on Mulberry Street* turned down by 27 publishers before his manuscript was accepted for publication. To date, 600 million Dr. Seuss books have been sold, with 11,000 Dr. Seuss books being sold every day of the year in the United States alone.
- The movie *Star Wars* was rejected by every movie studio in Hollywood before 20th Century-Fox produced it. It went on to gross $775 million, becoming one of the highest–grossing movies in film history.

What could *you* accomplish if you were to follow your heart, practice daily persistence, and never give up?

DISCOVERING MORE ABOUT YOU:
Your Track Record of Persistence

Consider this: You wouldn't be where you are today if you weren't already somewhat good at persisting. You probably already have a track record of enduring and overcoming challenges throughout your life. Some of your accomplishments required extra effort, others took a long time, and others were scary to pursue—but you achieved them anyway.

Your list of these achievements no doubt includes the basics required in life, such as studying even when it was boring, running farther than you thought you could, going to your first job interview, and so many bigger things since then.

In the spaces below, list three of the most significant times you persisted in the face of obstacles and challenges before reaching your goal. Recall those times when the going got tough, but you got tougher, and you persisted and succeeded.

Example: Think of a time when you persisted and reached your goal.

A. What was the challenge?

I was in a new sales job, and it was tough for me to
keep making sales calls when I wasn't getting results.

B. What did you do to persevere?

I knew I had to succeed, so I asked my sales manager for more help on my calls until
I learned the skills I needed. Because I kept at it, I got better with practice.

C. What did you achieve?

The second year I was named "Most Improved," although this was a consolation prize,
since I had done so poorly my first year. The fourth year, I became the #1 salesperson
in the company and made almost twice as much money as I ever had before.

D. What did you learn from this experience?

I learned that if I don't give up and I ask for help, I eventually succeed. I also learned
that when I persevere and win, my self-esteem and self-confidence improve.

1. Think of a time when you persisted and reached your goal.

A. What was the challenge?

_____

_____

_____

B. What did you do to persevere?

_____

_____

_____

C. What did you achieve?

_____

_____

_____

D. What did you learn from this experience?

_____

_____

_____

2. Think of another time when you persisted and reached your goal.

A. What was the challenge?

_____

_____

_____

B. What did you do to persevere?

_____

_____

_____

C. What did you achieve?

_____

_____

_____

D. What did you learn from this experience?

_____

_____

_____

3. Think of a third time when you persisted and reached your goal.

A. What was the challenge?

_____

_____

_____

B. What did you do to persevere?

_____

_____

_____

C. What did you achieve?

_____

_____

_____

D. What did you learn from this experience?

_____

_____

_____

Refer back to this track record of success to bolster yourself in the days ahead when you are faced with the inevitable challenges that will test your willingness to persist.

WRITE YOUR OWN SUCCESS STORY:
"How I Overcame Challenges to Reach My Breakthrough Goal"

You've probably heard this expression: The best way to predict your future is to create it. When you set your Breakthrough Goal and begin working toward it, you are working to create the future you most want. One of the ways to help ensure that future is by taking the time now to envision how you will overcome any of the challenges that may emerge along the way.

It's time to write your future success story using the questions and prompts below.

1. Review your Breakthrough Goal on page 72 in *Chapter 4: Use the Power of Goal-Setting to Achieve Your Vision.*

2. Describe an imagined moment in the future when you are so excited because you have just achieved your Breakthrough Goal—or some other crucial goal!

What's the date? _____

Imagine what exactly you have seen or heard that tells you that you have achieved your Breakthrough Goal.

_____
_____
_____

What is the strongest positive feeling you have as a result?

_____
_____
_____

How does this success change how you view yourself?

_____
_____
_____

3. Continuing to imagine you are in the future—and that you've reached your goal—describe the biggest challenge you had to overcome to get there—and how you overcame it.

_____
_____
_____

_____

_____

_____

_____

_____

Add to Your Life Success Journal

Turn to page 231 of *Your Life Success Journal* and complete the exercise for this chapter.

Transform
Yourself
for Success

Everyone thinks of changing the world,
but no one thinks of changing himself.

LEO TOLSTOY
Celebrated Russian Author

PRACTICE MEDITATION*

When you have achieved a state of deep meditation, you unlock the door to your subconscious mind. That is where the power to create the life you desire lies.

ADRIAN CALABRESE
Author of *How to Get Everything You Ever Wanted*

Decades of research show that meditation provides tremendous benefits in the areas of health and stress reduction. But for me, these benefits go even further: I meditate for 20 to 30 minutes most mornings, and have found that all the creative ideas and solutions I need to complete any task, solve any problem, or achieve any goal are all available inside me and will often appear while meditating.

When I was 35 years old, I attended a meditation retreat that changed my life forever. For an entire week, from 6:30 a.m. until 10:00 p.m.—with breaks only for meals and silent walks—we meditated. At first, I thought I might go crazy. Sometimes I fell asleep, and other times my mind would race from one topic to another as I reviewed almost every experience of my life, planned how to improve my business, and wondered what I was doing sitting in meditation while everyone else I knew was out enjoying their life.

However, on the fourth day, a beautiful thing happened. My mind became much quieter, and I moved to a place from which I could calmly witness everything that was occurring inside and around me without judgment or attachment. I had a profound sense of peace. I still had thoughts, but now they were deeper, more profound, and more insightful. I began to see connections I had never seen before. I understood my motivations, fears, and desires at a much deeper level. I became aware of creative solutions to problems I had been facing in my life. I felt more relaxed, calm, aware, and clear than I had ever felt before. When I focused

---

*Read *Principle 47: Inquire Within* in the book *The Success Principles* for more explanation, stories, and examples.

on my deepest, most heartfelt goals and desires, solutions would come pouring into my mind. I would see the steps I needed to take and the people I would need to speak with to overcome any obstacle. It was truly magical.

What I learned from this experience is that all the ideas I need to complete any task, solve any problem, or achieve any goal are all available inside of me. I've used meditation for centering, for stress reduction, and to access the wisdom and creativity of my subconscious and higher conscious mind ever since.

A regular meditation practice will help you achieve all of *your* goals more quickly and more effortlessly, too. It will help you clear out your mental and emotional distractions and provide you with valuable insights and ideas.

MEDITATION WORKS WONDERS

Using neuro-imaging and genomics technology to measure physiological changes in their subjects' brains and bodies, scientists at Harvard Medical School recently proved that meditation *boosts* the activity of genes involved in energy metabolism and insulin secretion—and reduces the activity of genes associated with inflammatory response and stress.

Better yet, just one session was enough to have a measurable positive effect—even for novices who had never meditated before.

In a separate study, Nobel Prize winner Elizabeth Blackburn and scientists at the University of California, Los Angeles found that 12 minutes of daily yoga meditation for eight weeks boosted telomerase activity by 43%. (Telomerase is also known as the "immortality enzyme" and has been proven to slow the cellular aging process.)

But the effects go far beyond your brain and body.

Meditation has also been scientifically proven to help you regulate emotions, decrease anxiety, increase your focus and attention, boost your self-control—and improve your ability to be creative and think outside the box.

Wouldn't those benefits help you significantly as you pursue your goals?

SOME FAMOUS MEDITATORS

But don't just take my word for it. Benjamin Franklin, Jerry Seinfeld, Tim Ferris, Deepak Chopra, and Madonna all meditate. So do Jim Carrey, Kristen Bell, Sting, the Beach Boys, and Bill Ford (executive chairman of the Ford Motor Company).

What do other successful people say who've made meditation part of their daily practice?

- Ray Dalio, billionaire hedge fund founder and author of *Principles*, says, "Meditation more than anything in my life was the biggest ingredient of whatever success I've had."
- Richard Gere, Golden Globe–winning actor, has been meditating for more than 40 years. He says, "It helps me set my motivation for the day."
- Eva Mendes, actress who has been meditating for 20-plus years, says, "I'm actually huge into meditation, . . . and that really helps create a sense of balance, . . . serenity, and kind of a calm state of mind."
- Tom Brady, six-time Super Bowl Champion quarterback for the New England Patriots, said he loves Transcendental Meditation.
- Tim Ryan, U. S. Congressman from Ohio, went on a five-day meditation retreat and has been hosting meditation sessions for members of Congress and their staff for years.
- Russell Simmons, cofounder of Def Jam Records, states, "You don't have to believe in meditation for it to work. You just have to take the time to do it. My advice? Meditate."
- Robert Stiller, billionaire founder of Keurig Green Mountain (the company behind the coffeemakers), said, "If you have a meditation practice, you can be much more effective in a meeting. Meditation helps develop your abilities to focus better and to accomplish your tasks."
- Katy Perry, one of the bestselling music artists of all time with an estimated net worth of $125 million, told *Marie Claire* magazine, "I start the day with Transcendental Meditation."
- Hugh Jackman, Golden Globe and Grammy-award winning actor, has been meditating for more than 20 years. He said, "In meditation, I can let go of everything. I'm not Hugh Jackman. I'm not dad. I'm not a husband. I'm just dipping into that powerful source that creates everything."

MEDITATION PREPARATION:
Time, Physical, Mental, and Environmental

In a moment, I will give you instructions for a beautiful, relaxing meditation. Before we get to that, here are some things to keep in mind to have a beneficial—and pleasant—experience.

- **Choosing the time to meditate.** I recommend meditating in the morning before you start your day. The benefit is that it helps you set a positive tone for the day. It raises your vibration, which will help keep your thoughts more positive and creative, your emotions more centered and less reactive, and your ability to stay focused stronger. Some people prefer to meditate at the end of the day as a way to relax, release stress, and transition to being present at home after work or as preparation for going to sleep. I also recommend writing the exact time you are going to meditate into your calendar or day planner. Research has shown that writing or typing it into your daily schedule significantly increases your chance of actually doing it.

- **Physical preparation.** Avoid meditating on a full stomach, when overly tired, or while wearing restrictive clothing. Do not meditate while under the influence of alcohol or drugs. Use your judgment when using prescribed medication.

- **Mental preparation.** It is helpful before meditation to prepare yourself mentally. For example, you may read, discuss, listen to, or think about something of an inspirational nature.

- **Environmental preparation.** Find a quiet time when you will not be disturbed by your phone, doorbell, children, or other interruptions. When you have moved into the inner stillness, all your senses are heightened, and a sudden noise can be a sudden shock to your system.

READY TO START? CLICK THESE LINKS AND I'LL GUIDE YOU THROUGH YOUR FIRST MEDITATION SESSIONS

Below you'll find written instructions on how to meditate, together with a link to a YouTube video in which I guide you through a basic meditation session. Once you're comfortable with meditation, consider purchasing *Awakening Power*, a set of my most powerful guided meditations, recorded with Dr. Deborah Sandella, where I further guide you through 11 different meditations (along with a 30-page study guide).

MEDITATION PROCESS:
Step-By-Step

Here is a simple process for beginning your meditation practice.

- Note the time. Meditate for at least 10 minutes when you are beginning. Work up to 20 minutes or more over time.

- Meditation can be done sitting cross-legged on the floor on a cushion, or as most people find more comfortable, sitting in a chair.

- Relax. It is helpful if your spine is straight. It is surprisingly easy to relax in an upright position if you will imagine a string tied to the top your head pulling straight up toward the ceiling.

- Gently close your eyes, if you're comfortable doing so. It is not required.

- Feel where your body touches the chair and the floor. Notice the sensations associated with sitting, such as pressure, or weight against the chair.

- Take a deep, slow breath, then another. Become aware of the sensations of breathing. Notice where you feel the breath—either at your nostrils, the expansion and contraction of your chest, or the rise and fall of your abdomen.

- Whenever your mind wanders, remember your breath, and gently return your awareness to the physical sensations of it.

- Remembering your breath, and returning your attention to it, is the practice. If you do that a hundred times, that is fine.

RECORDINGS OF GUIDED MEDITATIONS

To learn the meditations skills that I teach my students in my Breakthrough to Success Online program, I've recorded the following YouTube video where I provide instructions on how to meditate. In the second half of the video, I guide you through my Four-Part Meditation.

Visit JackCanfield.com/workbook-resources to access the video.

Breakthrough to Success Online

The Breakthrough to Success Online program includes sessions where I guide you through the following three meditations: The 4-Part Meditation, The Tree of Life Meditation, and the Disidentification Process Meditation. You can learn more about it and purchase the program at JackCanfield.com.

Awakening Power: A Complete Set of Guided Meditation Recordings

Another resource you can purchase at my Web site, these are some of my most powerful guided meditations and guided visualizations, recorded with Dr. Deborah Sandella. Visit JackCanfield.com.

MAKE-IT-A-HABIT WORKSHEET
Make Time to Meditate

1. Every day this week, meditate for at least 10 minutes. Over time, you may want to increase it to 20 minutes. Pay attention to your experience as you begin this new practice.

2. Set a reminder on your smartphone every day this week to practice mindfulness several times a day, if only for a moment. You can use the silent vibration mode on your phone, if you prefer.

3. Every day this week, locate one new resource for maintaining your meditation practice, whether an online meditation source, a local meditation group, a book, or a Web site to help you sustain your practice. See *Additional Meditation Resources* below.

ADDITIONAL MEDITATION RESOURCES

There are many resources available to help you learn meditation and to guide you in maintaining an ongoing meditation practice. A few of these include:

- Apps, such as *Insight Timer* (insighttimer.com) or *Headspace* (headspace.com).
- Web sites, such as UCLA's Mindful Awareness Research Center at www.ucla health.org/marc/mindful-meditations.

- Local Meetup groups and local meditation centers such as those affiliated with the Insight Meditation Society. Visit www.dharma.org/resources/meditation -centers-and-communities.
- Transcendental meditation. Visit TM.org.

Add to Your Life Success Journal

Turn to page 232 of *Your Life Success Journal* and complete the exercise for this chapter.

CLEAN UP YOUR MESSES
AND YOUR INCOMPLETES*

Clean up your own mess.

ROBERT FULGHUM
Author of *All I Really Need to Know I Learned in Kindergarten*

Successful achievers know the importance of releasing old, excess emotional baggage on their journey to success. They know it robs you of energy and is an ongoing distraction. Well, the same principle applies to *physical messes* that are left incomplete, as well as relationship issues that remain unresolved in your life.

Are there areas where you've left uncompleted projects or failed to get closure with people? The problem is that when you don't complete your past, you are not free to fully embrace the present or to easily create your future.

WHY DON'T PEOPLE COMPLETE?

Often, incompletions represent areas in our life where we're not clear—or where we have emotional or psychological blocks. For instance, you may have a lot of requests, projects, tasks, and other things on your desk that you want to say no to—but you're afraid of being perceived as selfish, insensitive, unappreciative, or uncooperative. So you put off responding to avoid saying no. Meanwhile the sticky notes and stacks of paper pile up and distract you from your more heartfelt goals. There may also be situations in which you need to make decisions that are

---

*Read *Principle 28: Clean Up Your Messes and Your Incompletes* in the book *The Success Principles* for more explanation, stories, and examples.

difficult or uncomfortable. Rather than deal with the discomfort, you let the in-completions pile up.

Other incompletes and messes come from not having adequate systems in place, or from not having the level of expertise for handling the necessary steps to complete the work. Other incompletions may pile up because of poor work habits.

Some incompletes are the result of overcommitting yourself to too many things, then not having the time you need to finish them. (With these, you may need to renegotiate with the people you committed to and take them off your plate. Or if that's not possible, you may need to delegate some or all of the work to others or hire someone to help you temporarily.)

Another reason for incompletes may be that you've decided you don't want to do a particular project, but you're afraid of offending the other person or people involved.

When you don't handle your "messes," they pile up and take your attention, thereby distracting you from what you do want to accomplish. Messes include things like an unresolved work situation, a messy garage, unfiled papers, an incomplete or contentious relationship, or something that needs to be organized or repaired. All of these messes also take your attention away from what we want to focus on, like our goals.

When you don't handle your incompletions, you may even go into resignation. When you put up with and tolerate something that is not working, you may find yourself thinking, *If I can't handle this little thing, how am I ever going to accomplish my bigger goals?* That mind-set can be devastating to your ability to achieve your goals.

COMPLETE THE TASK

One way to address your incompletes and messes is to complete the tasks that are in front of you. Continually ask yourself, *What would it take to get this task completed and off my back?* Then you can begin to consciously take one forward step, such as filing the completed documents, finishing the budget, or reporting back to your partner or your boss that the project is completed. It's far better to have one project completed than to have 5 projects hanging on and only partially done.

Sometimes completing the task means simply doing the work, as in the examples above. Other times, it may mean renegotiating the agreement around the task—or even deciding to give it up entirely and put it behind you, thereby declaring it "complete" (and off your plate) in your own mind. Are you allowed to simply give up and move past projects you wanted to do? Yes, you can do that! You are the one who gets to choose how to complete it—including abandoning it altogether—but complete it you must if you want all your energy and attention available to charge ahead toward achieving your Breakthrough Goal and other important goals you have set for yourself.

In a few moments, you'll have the chance to review some areas in your life where you may have tasks and situations that need completing.

DECLUTTER YOUR WORK AREAS AND LIVING AREAS

Many offices and households are groaning under the weight of too much clutter, too many papers, worn-out or never-worn clothes, unused toys and games, forgotten personal effects, obsolete and broken equipment, outdated technology, and other unneeded items.

Do you really need all that stuff? Of course not. One of the ways to free up your attention and focus is to free your work and living environments from the mental and visual burden of all this clutter. It's also important to remember that when you clear out the old, you're also making room for something new to come in.

If there's *anything* new that you want to add to your life, you have to make room for it. I mean that psychologically as well as physically. If you want a new love relationship in your life, you have to let go of (forgive and forget) the previous one(s) you were in—even if you haven't seen or talked to that person for over a year.

One way to support bringing in new business is to do what my friend Martin Rutte does. Whenever he wants new clients, he thoroughly cleans his office, home, car, and garage. Every single time he has done that, he starts hearing from people who want to work with him.

DISCOVERING MORE ABOUT YOU:
25 Areas to Complete, Dump, or Delegate Before Moving Forward

How many things do you need to complete, dump, or delegate before you can move on and bring new activity, abundance, relationships, and excitement into your life? Use the checklist below to jog your thinking and make a list of any incompletions or messes in your life that may be taking your time and attention away from you.

In the *Make-It-a-Habit* worksheet at the end of this chapter, you'll be asked to complete some of these items this week. The more you clear the old incompletes out of your life, the more space you create for new successes to enter your life. Commit to how often and when you will review and resolve the incompletions in your life, and then add those dates to your calendar. Let's start by taking the time to make a complete list of your current incompletions.

What incompletions do you have regarding:

1. Former business activities
2. Promises not kept, not acknowledged, or not renegotiated
3. Unpaid debts or financial commitments; money owed to others or money owed to you
4. Closets overflowing with clothing never worn
5. A disorganized garage or basement crowded with old discards
6. Haphazard or disorganized tax records
7. Checkbook not balanced or accounts you should close
8. "Junk drawers" full of unusable items
9. Broken tools
10. An attic filled with unused items that have no real or sentimental value
11. A car trunk or back seat full of trash
12. Overdue car maintenance
13. Incomplete home-renovation projects
14. Credenza packed or stacked with obsolete material or unrealized projects
15. Filing left undone
16. Computer files not backed up or organized
17. Desk surface cluttered or disorganized
18. Family pictures never put into an album or a digital file
19. Mending, ironing, or items to repair, donate, or discard
20. Deferred household maintenance
21. Personal relationships with unstated resentments or past-due appreciations
22. People you need to forgive
23. Time not spent with people you've meant to spend time with
24. Incomplete projects or projects delivered without closure or feedback
25. Acknowledgments that need to be given or asked for

For larger projects like cleaning out your garage or basement, you may want to enlist the aid of friends. You can always return the favor by helping them out for a day in return. You may also want to find a professional organizer to assist you. Here is a link to the National Association of Productivity & Organizing Professionals where you can locate someone in your area: Napo.net.

WHAT'S IRRITATING YOU?

Like incompletes, daily irritants are equally damaging to your success because they, too, take up your attention and focus. Perhaps it's the missing button on your favorite suit that keeps you from wearing it to an important meeting or the torn screen on your patio door that lets in annoying insects. One of the best things you can do to move further and faster along your path to success is to fix, replace, mend, or get rid of those daily irritants that annoy you and take up valuable space in your mind.

Make a list of the things that irritate you and the things you are tolerating on the next page. Use additional sheets of paper if your list is long.

MY IRRITATIONS & TOLERATIONS LIST

What Is Irritating Me?	How Can I Fix It?	Who Can I Delegate All or Part of Fixing It To?	Due Date
Example: Email	Respond, unsubscribe, or trash.	Ask my assistant to help me for one hour a week.	Begin this Friday
Example: Proposals taking too long	Create a template to reuse.	Ask for ideas from my mastermind group.	Next mastermind meeting
Example: My negative self-talk	Surround myself with positive and successful people.	Attend a business booster Meetup.	Tuesday evening

Take yourself through the following questions for each item on your list above. It's even more powerful if you allow someone, like your accountability partner, to take you through the questions.

1. What irritates you?
2. What do you need to do to fix it?
3. Who could you ask to help get it handled?
4. How do you stop yourself from asking?
5. What is the possible benefit of asking?
6. When will you ask?

THE 6-STAGE TOTAL TRUTH PROCESS: RESOLVE INCOMPLETE RELATIONSHIPS AND RELEASE NEGATIVE EMOTIONS FROM THE PAST

When you go through life with unresolved hurt feelings, resentments, or anger, it's as if you're dragging a big anchor behind you, weighing and slowing you down. Perhaps you're holding on to anger toward a past partner, friend, or employer. If you could release it, you would be able to move faster and succeed more easily. The truth is, you need to let go of the past to embrace the future. One method I recommend for this is the Total Truth Process.

This is a tool to help you release negative emotions and return to a more resourceful state of appreciation, love, and joy. The process is not intended to let you "dump" or discharge negative feelings onto someone else, but to take responsibility for your emotions as you fully express them and experience them to the other person—either in person or in writing. The goal is to express your anger, resentment, hurt, and fear, and replace it with understanding, compassion, forgiveness, peace, and love. You may wish to have the other person participate, too, in order to help them release their own negative emotions about what happened.

DISCOVERING MORE ABOUT YOU:
The 6-Stage Total Truth Process

The Total Truth Process can be conducted verbally or in writing using the six prompts listed below. If the other person is not someone likely to agree to cooperate in this process, you may choose to write the letter and then throw it away once you have completed it. The primary purpose is to free you from the unexpressed emotions. If you can do the process in person, that's great. If not, just identifying and expressing your feelings on paper can be extremely valuable.

Letter to (name of person) _____

I'm angry that _____

_____

_____.

I felt hurt when _____

_____

_____.

I'm afraid that (or I feel scared when) _____

_____

_____.

I'm sorry that I (this is where you want to own anything that you might have done that might have contributed to the event or the situation) _____

_____

_____.

I want you to _____

_____

_____.

I forgive you for _____

_____

_____.

I love you and I appreciate you for _____

_____

_____.

MAKE-IT-A-HABIT WORKSHEET
Take Action on Cleaning Up Your
Messes and Your Incompletes

Each day this week, take the opportunity to put one or two activities from this chapter into practice. Place a check mark to the right side of the activity when you have completed it.

Day 1: Select at least one mess or incomplete, then take steps to resolve it.

Mess selected: _____ Check when completed: ____

Day 2: Write a 6-Stage Total Truth Letter (even if you don't intend to send it).

Person selected: _____ Check when completed: ____

Day 3: Select at least one mess or incomplete, then take steps to resolve it.

Mess selected: _____ Check when completed: ____

Day 4: Write a 6-Stage Total Truth Letter (even if you don't intend to send it).

Person selected: _____ Check when completed: ____

Day 5: Select at least one mess or incomplete, then take steps to resolve it.

Mess selected: _____ Check when completed: ____

Day 6: Select at least one mess or incomplete, then completely resolve it.

Mess selected: _____ Check when completed: ____

Day 7: Select at least one mess or incomplete, then completely resolve it.

Mess selected: _____ Check when completed: ____

Add to Your Life Success Journal

Turn to page 233 of *Your Life Success Journal* and complete the exercise for this chapter.

PART THREE

Build Your Success Team

None of us is as smart as all of us.

KEN BLANCHARD
Leadership Guru and Author of *The One Minute Manager*

CHAPTER

14

SURROUND YOURSELF WITH
SUCCESSFUL PEOPLE*

You are the average of the five people you spend the most time with.

JIM ROHN
Author of *Take Charge of Your Life*

One of the facts of life is that you become like the people you spend the most time with. They impact the way you think, the way you feel, and the way you act. Think about the people you know or are aware of: the negative people tend to hang out with other negative people, and the positive people spend time with other positive people. The successful and wealthy people tend to hang out with other successful and wealthy people—and the same goes for those who are health conscious and those who are not. Straight-A students tend to hang out with other straight-A students. Officers congregate with other officers, enlisted men with the enlisted men, and so on. The point is that it's *critically* important to intentionally choose those people you're spending time with—since you'll tend to take on the mind-set, motivations, and even mannerisms of those people.

If you want to be more successful, you need to spend more time with people who are already successful and with people who are equally committed to becoming as successful as you are. You need to surround yourself with other positive, encouraging, solution-oriented, possibility thinkers.

Choose to spend more time with those friends and colleagues who are successful, positive, and supportive of your goals. You can also join groups and go to events that include people who've found success in the areas in which you are interested. There are numerous professional associations, conferences, local Meetup groups of like-minded people (www.meetup.com), civic groups such as Rotary

---

*Read *Principle 25: Drop Out of the "Ain't It Awful" Club . . . and Surround Yourself with Successful People* in the book *The Success Principles* for more explanation, stories, and examples.

and Kiwanis, or groups for entrepreneurs and business owners like the Young Entrepreneurs Organization and Vistage.

If you're self-employed in a one-person business, there are coworking spaces in most cities where you can rent a desk or an office and work around other aspiring solopreneurs. You can also attend lectures, workshops, courses, trainings, boot camps, and retreats that are conducted by those who have already achieved what you want to achieve and that are attended by people who are equally committed to growing themselves, their careers, and their businesses. There are also women's groups for moms, nonprofit managers, senior executives, Millennial women, and Baby Boomers. One women's movement we especially like is GoalFriends: local small groups that hold "parties with a purpose" once a month so women can celebrate each others' wins, study a goal-setting curriculum, and hold each other accountable to achieve milestones every month.★

FIND A MENTOR OR A COACH

You would also be wise to find a mentor or a coach who can assist you by sharing what they know. They also have both the expertise and experience of having worked with people just like you helping *them* to get to where they want to be.

Mentors are people who've already accomplished what you want to do. They can help you clarify your purpose and your goals, plan for success, make better decisions, challenge your limiting beliefs, and so much more.

If you're an entrepreneur or a business owner, you can access a business mentor for your small business—at no cost—through SCORE, the U.S. network of volunteer, expert business mentors, with over 10,000 volunteers in 300 chapters around the country. Many of the mentors are retired executives with vast experience. You can access ongoing mentoring in person, via email or by videoconference. Learn more by going to Score.org.

Hiring a life coach or a business coach can also save you years of misdirected effort, as well as the frustration of trying to discover winning practices in your field on your own. With a business coach, you're much more likely to achieve

---

★You can learn more about GoalFriends at GoalFriend.com.

your personal, professional, business and revenue goals sooner, as well as reduce your expenses along the way. Here are a few suggestions that you can check out.

- Canfield Coaching at JackCanfield.com/coaching
- Strategic Coach with Dan Sullivan at StrategicCoach.com
- Action Coaching at ActionCoach.com
- The International Coaching Federation at CoachFederation.com

LISTEN AND LEARN

Another way to spend time with successful people is to take advantage of the amazing books, podcasts, and videos produced by successful people—learning their proven strategies and becoming inspired by their success. Here are some that I listen to and highly recommend to you:

The School of Greatness with Lewis Howes
Eventual Millionaire with Jaime Tardy
The Tim Ferriss Show with Tim Ferriss
Find Your Amazingness with Veera Markkanen
Extreme Productivity with Kevin Kruse
Girlboss Radio with Sophia Amoruso
Getting Things Done with David Allen
The Science of Success with Matt Bodnar
The Creative Empire with Reina Pomeroy & Christina Scalera
Entrepreneur on Fire with John Lee Dumas

Also, go to player.fm/podcasts/Success-on-the-Internet, where literally hundreds of podcasts are listed, and many are focused on specific populations such as success for women, solo entrepreneurs, small business owners, startups, real estate investors, farmers, and crowdsourcing fund-raisers.

INTERVIEW SUCCESSFUL PEOPLE

There are also successful people all around you from whom you could learn—you just have to look for them and take the first step to reach out to them. Most people, however, will never take that first step—which is why most people still struggle to reach success.

I was once asked to speak at a sales meeting for a company that manufactures optical lenses. I asked, "How many of you know who the top five salespeople in the company are?" Almost everyone raised their hand. Then I asked, "How many of you have ever approached one of these top five salespeople and asked them to share their secrets of success with you?" Not one hand went up. Seriously!

So why don't people take advantage of an amazing resource that is just a phone call, a cubicle, or a lunch conversation away? The answer for most people is that they fear rejection. They fear that the person will say, "No, I don't want to share that with you."

Well, as I already revealed in *Chapter 9* of this *Workbook*, you really have nothing to lose and everything to gain by asking. If they say no, you're no worse off than before you asked them. You didn't know the answer then, and you don't know it now. Your life didn't get worse. And if they say yes, you have the chance of learning some valuable information.

Think about some of the successful people around you (at work, in your family, in your neighborhood, in your club, in your church or temple, or in your civic groups) that you could reach out to and ask.

SUCCESS THROUGH LEARNING FROM OTHERS

When Emile Labadie became an agent for the Wilson Learning Corporation selling management training programs, he was new to sales. However, he had one particular, rare trait that led him to success—and wealth. He was on the phone almost daily with the most successful salespeople in the company. Emile would ask them how they were selling a new program, or how they overcame specific common objections, or how they were able to reach a decision-maker at a client company who was in a higher position with greater buying power.

But Emile didn't just take: He would make sure that he was giving away his discoveries and best practices to the others at the same time. Emile made himself into a valued resource to the most successful—and the not–so–successful—people in the business. Besides learning from those who were selling the same products as he was, he would also reach out to people working in other companies that were related in some way to find out what was working for them. He worked as hard at helping others be successful as he was at helping himself. (Well, almost.) He always wanted to be at the top of the sales ranking, make the most money, and win every sales contest. Most of the time, he did.

If you are going to be successful, you have to start spending time with successful people. You need to ask them to share their success strategies with you. You need to try out those strategies and see if they work for you. Experiment with doing what they do, reading what they read, thinking the way they think, and so on. If their way of thinking and behaving seems like it might work for you, adopt their mind-set and actions and see what happens. If not, keep looking, experimenting, and paying attention to the feedback to find what works for you.

DISCOVERING MORE ABOUT YOU:
Your Current and Future Groups

Evaluate Your Current Group

In the space below, list the five or more people you spend the most time with and evaluate their benefit or hindrance to your progress and success.*

In the second column, place a "+" if the person is a positive influence, a "0" if they are neutral, or a "−" if they are mainly a negative influence.

Name		How She/He Contributes to My Success	How He/She Hinders My Success
Emily M.	+	She runs her own social media marketing company, and she is always so positive and willing to offer ideas.	
Mike C.	−		He appears professional, but I have seen him be dishonest.

*Duplicate this page if you wish to add more people.

With Whom Would You Rather Spend Time?

Now that you have identified those who contribute to your success—and those who don't—you have the opportunity to revise your list of those with whom you want to spend time. After all, this is your life and your success. In the space below, list those with whom you would like to spend more time. They can replace those you identified above who tend to hinder your success.

Name	How She/He Could Contribute to My Success or Growth	How Will I Approach This Person?	By When
Will E.	He has his own successful coaching business and could give me advice.	I could ask Sasha to introduce us via email or phone.	2/23
			/
			/
			/
			/
			/
			/
			/
			/
			/
			/
			/
			/

Your Ideal Mentors

Create a list of at least 10 people you can think of, or unknown people with specific skills, from whom you could learn the most.

Name	What I Want to Learn from Him/Her	By When
Karen G.	She launched a podcast, and I could ask her how she was able to get noteworthy people to be guests on her show.	12/11
(Unknown person)	Find someone who has published an e-book to learn about the tools they recommend for formatting a book.	12/11
		/
		/
		/
		/
		/
		/
		/
		/
		/
		/
		/
		/

Groups to Explore

No matter where you live, there are probably groups meeting nearby that could benefit you and contribute to your success. Some may offer support and/or expertise. To locate groups, try a Google search, or view lists of meetings at Meetup.com. Fill in your answers below.

What Would Be Helpful to You?	Local Group to Check Out and Maybe Join	By When
Improve my ability to speak to groups	Toastmasters	2/7
How to start a podcast	Local Meetup about podcasting, listed at Meetup .com	2/19
		/
		/
		/
		/
		/
		/
		/
		/
		/
		/
		/
		/

Make an Appointment

Each day this week, call one person on the list above and ask if they would be willing to share their knowledge and experience with you. Schedule a meeting time with each person who agrees.

Name	When We Will Meet
Karen G.	She said yes! We will meet this Friday at her home office—and she will show me her recording setup, too!
1.	
2.	
3.	
4.	
5.	
6.	
7.	

Add to Your Life Success Journal

Turn to page 234 of *Your Life Success Journal* and complete the exercise for this chapter.

CHAPTER

15

START A MASTERMIND GROUP AND WORK WITH AN ACCOUNTABILITY PARTNER*

The Mastermind principle consists of an alliance of two or more minds working in perfect harmony for the attainment of a common definite objective. Success does not come without the cooperation of others.

NAPOLEON HILL
Author of *Think and Grow Rich*

One of the most powerful tools used by successful people is the *mastermind group*—a close-knit alliance of five or six people who meet regularly to help each other succeed more quickly and more easily. How? By brainstorming solutions to each other's challenges and problems, sharing valuable resources with each other, encouraging each other to stretch and grow, keeping each other motivated, and holding each other accountable to taking those actions they've committed to pursuing.

In this chapter, you'll learn how to locate, evaluate, and join the right mastermind group, or create one of your own. You'll also learn the six-step structure for efficient and effective mastermind group meetings that will ensure everyone gets maximum value from the meetings—a factor that ensures the group will stay together because all the members are getting a benefit. You will also read a step-by-step outline for successfully conducting your first and subsequent mastermind group meetings.

In addition to joining a mastermind group, I also recommend you work with an *accountability partner*. This is a trusted colleague who agrees to hold you accountable to the daily tasks and longer-term goals you're working on. Knowing you have to "report in" to someone you respect is a potent motivator for avoiding

---

*Read *Principle 46: Mastermind Your Way to Success* in the book *The Success Principles* for more explanation, stories, and examples.

distractions, eliminating procrastination, and maintaining your focus on completing those specific tasks that will lead to the achievement of your most important goals.

If you want to go fast, go alone.
If you want to go far, go together.
AFRICAN PROVERB

YOUR MASTERMIND GROUP

A mastermind group is a structure for accelerating both your personal and professional growth, as well as the achievement of your goals.

A mastermind group is made up of people who come together regularly—weekly, biweekly, or monthly—to share ideas, thoughts, information, feedback, contacts, and resources. The group can focus on business issues, personal issues, or both. For a mastermind group to be powerfully effective, people must be committed to tell each other the truth about what they want to accomplish, where they are stuck or challenged, and what their needs are. Some of the most valuable feedback I have ever received has come from members of my mastermind group confronting me about overcommitting, selling my services too cheaply, focusing on the trivial, not delegating enough, thinking too small, and playing it safe.

Members must also be committed to play full out with each other in terms of sharing their best ideas and resources, and also maintaining the confidentiality of what one shares in the group.

HOW TO ASSEMBLE A MASTERMIND GROUP

Choose people who are already at a level where you'd like to be in your life—or who are at least one or two levels above you. You're probably wondering why they would want to be involved in a group with you. The answer is because they are not in a mastermind group, and you are the one organizing it and putting it together.

Although the size can vary, the ideal size I have found for a mastermind group is five or six people. That way, each person will be able to have a chance to ask for and receive the support they need at each meeting, yet the sessions will still have a reasonable duration—usually one hour. If the group is any smaller than six people, if one or two people are sick—or unable to attend due to travel or a family emergency—the group loses its dynamic power.

If you do not want to start your own group, consider joining an existing group. To find a local group, search online for "mastermind group" plus the area where you live. You can expand your search using the keywords "business networking" instead for organizations that may also offer mastermind groups. You can also search at Meetup.com for local meetings. If you prefer an online option, you can search using similar keywords, without a location.

How to Conduct Your Mastermind Meeting

As you start your mastermind group, keep in mind these proven guidelines as you plan for your first meeting.

1. All members should attend all meetings.
2. Meetings can be conducted in person, over the telephone (using a service, such as FreeConference.com or UberConference.com, that features screen-sharing) or using a videoconference service such as Zoom or Skype.
3. Most people find that meeting every two weeks seems to be the optimal time. These meetings must be held as a top priority by all the members.
4. The ideal length of time is 60 to 90 minutes. Set a time and strictly adhere to it at each meeting.
5. Each meeting should have a designated timekeeper. It is vital that everyone gets his or her allotted amount of time and that you stick to the schedule. This is important if you want your group to last. Otherwise, meetings can drag on, and members will eventually lose interest and quit.
6. As each member joins the group, he or she should familiarize the others with their major goals, current situation, and their current opportunities, needs, and challenges. This will allow the other members, in future meetings, to better ask the right questions and effectively brainstorm ways to support them. During the first meeting of the group, all the members should do this.

7. Each member needs to agree to play full out—to openly share ideas, support, contacts, information, honest feedback, and anything else that will help advance the individual and group goals. This also means that every member should come to each meeting prepared to share his or her current challenges and requests for help—which occasionally are highly personal.

8. One last guideline: If everyone has only 10 or 20 minutes to be the focus (depending on how long you have chosen to meet for), avoid the trap of spending too much time detailing the problem or the request, and make sure to leave enough time for brainstorming and suggestions.

RECOMMENDED AGENDA

Here are the best practices for conducting the actual meeting (together with the recommended time limit for each).

Step 1: Invocation (1 minute)
If the other members agree to it, start your meetings with an invocation—asking whatever Higher Power you believe in to be present and guide everyone to be fully present, ready to play full out, and to say and do only that which is for the highest good of each member in the group. You could also start with a prayer, an inspiring story, or an inspirational quotation. It is best to rotate this function to a different member each time and to let them do it in their own way.

Step 2: Share What's New and Good (1 minute for each person)
Start by having each member share something positive and good that has happened since the last meeting. This can also include reporting on any actions they committed to take at the previous meeting.

Step 3: Negotiate for Time (a total of 2 minutes or less for the group)
Each person should ask for a certain amount of time to discuss their issues. Usually you can agree to divide the available time equally, but there may be times when certain members feel strongly that they need more time for an important issue or emerging crisis they are facing. Also, if not everyone wants a turn, they can allocate their time back to the group so each person needing time can have a bit more.

Step 4: Individual Members Speak While the Group Listens and Then Brainstorms Solutions (7 to 10 minutes for each person)

Each person has the amount of time negotiated and agreed to. They spend the first few moments of their time sharing the matter at hand for them—their problem, challenge, opportunity, need, or request—followed by asking for specific support such as ideas, solutions, resources, introductions, or something else. For the rest of their allotted time, the individual listens to the ideas and suggestions presented by the other members. It's best not to spend too much time describing the challenge or the need so that there is enough time to hear possible solutions. It is also a good idea not to argue with the suggestions. Just listen and take notes.

Step 5: Make a Commitment to Act (30 seconds or less per person)

Each member commits to one or more actions they will take by the next meeting—based on the feedback and suggestions they've received from the group.

Step 6: End with Gratitude/Share Appreciations (2 to 3 minutes total for the group)

The meeting ends with each person sharing appreciations and acknowledgments to the people who contributed solutions. (For example: "Joe, I really appreciate your willingness to introduce me to the president of the bank. Jolene, I really appreciate your two ideas on how to handle that difficult client.")

The Last Step: Make sure everyone is clear about and committed to the next meeting time before you get off the call.

MY MEETING PLAN FOR MY MASTERMIND GROUP MEETING★

Week of _____

Challenges or Projects to Share with the Group:

_____

_____

_____

_____

_____

_____

_____

_____

_____

Suggestions from the Group:

_____

_____

_____

_____

_____

_____

_____

_____

Contacts/People/Resources Suggested by Group:

_____

_____

_____

_____

_____

_____

_____

_____

Areas to Take Action On:

_____

_____

_____

_____

_____

_____

_____

_____

★Please print or photocopy this form for you and the other members' ongoing use.

ACCOUNTABILITY PARTNERS

Having an accountability partner is one of the most powerful ways to ensure that you actually take the actions—especially the uncomfortable ones—necessary to achieve the successes you want, such as achieving the big Breakthrough Goal you set earlier in this *Workbook*.

When you have an accountability partner, the two of you agree to talk regularly by phone or videoconference to hold each other accountable for taking the actions you need to take, meeting your deadlines, and accomplishing your goals. Use texting only as a last resort.

To get the most benefit out of the relationship, you should agree to speak with each other at agreed-upon times (I recommend every workday, preferably in the morning) to share your top five action steps for the day, and hold each other accountable for the previous day's five commitments. The simple fact that you are being held accountable to someone on a daily basis provides a significant extra incentive to get the job done. This is especially useful if you're a solo entrepreneur (such as a consultant, an author, a coach, an Internet marketer, or a service provider), or if you're a salesperson, or you work from home. In turn, you will provide the accountability that *your partner* needs to reach his or her own goals.

An accountability partner can also provide enthusiasm and encouragement when yours is waning because of the obstacles, distractions, setbacks, or failures you are facing. The key to a successful accountability relationship is choosing someone who is as excited about reaching their goals as you are about reaching yours, who's intensely committed to your (and their own) success, and who has enough personal power to be able to confront you, hold you accountable, and support you when you are not following through on your commitments.

HOW TO CHOOSE A GOOD ACCOUNTABILITY PARTNER

So who should you choose as an accountability partner? The answer to this varies dramatically based on your circumstances and your goals. Accountability can come from anyone, such as friends with similar goals, colleagues at work, mentors, coaches, or personal advisors. One caution: I usually don't advise having your spouse or a close family member as your accountability partner. These relationships have the disadvantage of having historical baggage and sometimes dysfunctional relational patterns that can get in the way of your staying neutral with each other.

Questions for Interviewing an Accountability Partner

You will have greater success in finding the right accountability partner if you use the following questions to interview the people you're considering. You will want to answer the same questions for them if you agree to work together.

- Tell me about yourself (basic biographical information).
- How much time shall we commit to our calls?
- What times of the day works best for you?
- Do you consider yourself to be left-brained (analytical) or right-brained (creative)?
- Are you someone who plans or do you have a tendency to wait until the last minute?
- What motivates you?
- When you've set goals in the past, what worked to keep you focused and moving forward when you were met with obstacles or weren't achieving as much success as you wanted?
- What is the best way to give you feedback that allows you to stay open and receptive to the feedback? If you get defensive or scared, what is the best way to respond so I don't support you in staying stuck?
- What do I need to know about you that might present challenges for our relationship?
- What do I need to know about you that will support our relationship?

Guidelines for Accountability Check-Ins

If you want to get the maximum value from your accountability partnership, it's essential to follow these guidelines.

1. Agree to connect at a specific time on specific days. The best strategy is to connect every workday, typically Monday through Friday.

2. In most cases, it's best to connect by phone or by videoconference on Zoom or Skype. When that's impossible for whatever reason, it's still essential to connect by text or email, whichever is most convenient for you.

3. Limit the call to five minutes. If the call goes longer, the process becomes tedious and inefficient, and one member or the other may want to quit.

4. During the call, each person takes a couple of minutes to report on whether or not they completed the action steps they had committed to the previous day, and what action steps they are committed to complete today.

5. I recommended that you use the Rule of 5 (See *Chapter 7: Take Action!* in this *Workbook*) and identify 5 specific actions you will complete by the next call.

6. Don't make excuses. When reporting on the previous day's commitments, just say whether or not you took the actions or completed the tasks you committed to. Your partner should then do the same. Don't waste time discussing excuses for why you or your partner didn't get something completed. Just ask if they are willing to recommit to it today, asking, "Are you willing to commit to taking that action today?"

7. If a task is not completed after several days in a row, you can ask what's coming up for them or what's getting in the way that might be stopping them. It could be fear or a limiting belief, or they may lack the necessary information, knowledge, resources, or courage to proceed. You can also ask if the action they are avoiding taking is something they really want to do, or is it something they merely think they "should" do. Sometimes it's better to delete it unless it's something critical to the achievement of an important goal. You can also take a few minutes to *briefly* explore if there is some support they might need from you or someone else.

8. During the call, either of you can suggest any resources such as books, TED talks, podcasts, seminars, online courses, YouTube videos, and people you are aware of who you think might be useful to them.

9. Get off the call once you complete. Do not allow it to shift into a casual social conversation. Schedule that for another time if you both agree you want to do it.

10. To ensure the calls remain valuable, from time to time you can ask the question, "On a scale of one to ten, how would you rate the value of these calls?" Any answer less than a 10 gets the follow-up question: "What would have to happen to make it a ten?"

Add to Your Life Success Journal

Turn to page 235 of *Your Life Success Journal* and complete the exercise for this chapter.

PART FOUR

Create Successful Relationships

The greatest compliment that was ever paid to me was when someone asked me what I thought, and attended to my answer.

HENRY DAVID THOREAU
American Philosopher, Essayist, and Poet

HAVE A HEART TALK*

Listen a hundred times. Ponder a thousand times. Speak once.

SOURCE UNKNOWN

Any relationship can benefit from the open and honest expression of what one is thinking and feeling, and the opportunity to speak without interruption. Healthy relationships are a key component of both your personal and professional success. But how do you structure a conversation so that you and others can be open and honest, and feel free to express their thoughts and feelings?

The answer is a Heart Talk.

A Heart Talk can be between you and your significant other, with your family, with a group at work, or with any group of people with whom you have regular contact and that would benefit from more open and honest communication and the authentic expression of feelings.

A SIMPLE HEART-BASED TOOL TO IMPROVE LIFE AT HOME AND WORK

A Heart Talk is a powerful communication process that creates a safe environment for a deep level of communication to occur—without fear of condemnation, unsolicited advice, interruption, or of being rushed. It's an incredibly effective way to release any unexpressed thoughts or emotions that get in the way of people being totally present and authentic with one another and working harmoniously and productively together as a team.

---

*Read *Principle 49: Have a Heart Talk* in the book *The Success Principles* for more explanation, stories, and examples.

Plus it's the best way I know to develop intimacy and understanding among members of a family or individuals in a group—and turn apparent adversaries into collaborators. As you foster more open communication within your family, friendships, and work groups, you will notice several changes right away.

1. People become more aware of each other's feelings.

Most people are so focused on what they're doing and what's happening to them, that they often don't stop to think about how their words or actions might impact others.

Heart Talks encourage the open sharing of feelings, giving family and team members deeper insight into what's happening in the lives of the others. This encourages greater empathy, more mindful communication, better solutions, and a deeper level of mutual respect in the home and in the workplace.

2. People don't take things as personally.

When you cultivate an environment of open and honest communication, people are less likely to read implied negative meaning into other people's words and actions. If someone is having a particularly stressful day, they are less likely to say or do something that's thoughtless or impatient. Others will be better able to understand that what's said is not about *them*, and they'll be less likely to feel hurt or resentful about it.

3. People feel more comfortable saying what they really think about you, your behavior, and how it affects them.

Too often, others will remain silent about problems they see because they don't want to add to the conflict or be seen as being critical. This often means that those who are closest to you and your projects, and who might be better able to anticipate problems, don't speak up. By encouraging open and honest communication, you make it safe for others you care about to say what they really think—instead of what they believe you want them to say.

When people become more vulnerable and authentic with each other, it increases their understanding and compassion for each other, which helps create an

environment of mutual trust and respect. The result is more peace and cooperation at home and more achievement in the workplace.

4. At work, you dramatically reduce staff turnover.

People who work or volunteer in an environment where they feel safe, heard,
cared for, and respected—interacting every day with people they like and whose
company they truly enjoy—know they've hit the jackpot. They are very reluctant
to leave such a supportive environment to pursue other opportunities. This allows
you to grow a team whose long history of open communication ensures they
work like a well-oiled machine, and relieves you of the need to invest precious
time, money, and resources in training new employees or volunteer staff.

> *Personal relationships are the fertile soil from which all advancement,*
> *all success, all achievement in real life grows.*
>
> BEN STEIN
> Former Speechwriter for Two U.S. Presidents

HOW TO CONDUCT A HEART TALK

Follow these steps to ensure a successful and meaningful Heart Talk. First, determine whom to include, and invite them to participate. Once everyone has gath-
ered, have them sit in a circle or around a table. Next, select an object for the
group to use to indicate who has the floor. We use a velvet heart-shaped beanbag
in our company because it is soft and comforting and reminds everyone not only
that what they are hearing is coming from the other person's heart but also that
everyone involved is trying to get to the heart of the matter at hand. However, any
object can work, such as a ball, a paperweight, or a stuffed animal like a teddy bear,
so long as it will be visible in the hands or lap of the participant who is speaking.

A time estimate should be decided upon and agreed to. If it is just two people,
allow ten to fifteen minutes, or longer if it is an emotionally intense issue. If the
group is three or more people, plan for about five to eight minutes per person.

List on a flip chart (or pass out copies of) the following "Guidelines for a Successful Heart Talk" and read them through together. Make sure everyone understands and agrees to the guidelines.

EIGHT GUIDELINES FOR A SUCCESSFUL HEART TALK

1. Only the person holding the "heart" talks. Everyone else just listens. Do not interrupt, question, or argue with the person who is talking.
2. Pass the heart gently to the left after your turn.
3. You may choose to "pass" when it is your turn.
4. Talk about how you feel as well as what you think about the topic at hand.
5. Do not judge or criticize what anyone else has said. Listen with an open mind with the intention of understanding the other person's experience.
6. Keep all information that is shared during the group confidential. No gossiping about what happened or who said what.
7. Do not leave the Heart Talk until it is declared complete by the leader.
8. Be considerate of how long you talk. Make sure everyone gets a turn.

Show the group the heart or object you will be using to pass around. Next determine who will go first. (You can lighten the mood by suggesting something fun like "whoever is wearing the most pieces of jewelry" or "whoever has the longest or shortest hair.") Once you begin, when a person finishes speaking, they always pass the heart to the next person on the left. That provides a sense of predictability, safety, and structure to the group.

Keep passing the heart/object around the circle—multiple times, if necessary—to ensure participants have more than one opportunity to share if they need it. If you only have a set amount of time, be sure to end on time, but make sure everyone has had at least one turn to share. If you have enough time, a Heart Talk completes naturally when the heart makes a complete circle without anyone having anything else to say—that is, everyone says, "I pass."

If you are leading the Heart Talk, make sure everyone sticks to the guidelines and doesn't interrupt anyone else while they are speaking. Sticking to the guidelines is what makes it a safe space for people to share what they are really thinking and feeling.

I strongly believe that you can't win in the marketplace
unless you win first in the workplace. If you don't have a winning culture
inside, it's hard to compete in the very tough world outside.

DOUGLAS CONANT
Fortune 500 Leadership Icon Who Previously Served as Chairman of Avon Products,
CEO of Campbell Soup Company,
and President of Nabisco Foods

SOME GOOD TIMES TO HAVE A HEART TALK

- When there is a conflict between people or departments
- When someone has been injured, is very ill, or has died
- During a challenging financial crisis
- When people are unclear about the vision, goal, or objective of a project
- Before or after a downsizing, merger, or acquisition
- When there is a new owner, boss, or manager
- As part of a long staff meeting or corporate retreat
- After a major disappointment like a failure to make an important sale, get a contract, or achieve an objective
- When someone important to the group has been fired or has left the group
- After a traumatic event such as 9/11 or a mass shooting

Some Common Topics That Are Useful

- What are you most concerned about in regard to . . . ?
- What is the greatest challenge you are facing right now?
- What are you all feeling about . . . ?
- What do you need to say before we move forward with this plan?

What Kind of Results Can You Expect?

After you conduct a Heart Talk, you can expect the following results:

- Enhanced listening skills
- Constructive expression of feelings
- Improved conflict resolution skills
- Improved ability to let go of resentments and old issues
- Development of mutual respect and understanding
- Greater sense of connection, unity, and bonding

The structure of a Heart Talk creates a safe, nonjudgmental space that supports the constructive—rather than the destructive—expression of feelings that, if left unexpressed, can block teamwork, synergy, creativity, innovation, and intuition, all of which are vital to the emotional health of a family or team and to the success of any venture.

DISCOVERING MORE ABOUT YOU:
Who Should You Ask to Have a Heart Talk?

Make a list of specific people you interact with and groups you belong to who you think would benefit from having a Heart Talk.

1. Individuals whom you would like to invite to have a one-to-one Heart Talk:

_____   _____

_____   _____

_____   _____

2. Groups you belong to where you would like to suggest having a group Heart Talk:

_____   _____

_____   _____

_____   _____

MAKE-IT-A-HABIT WORKSHEET
Schedule a Heart Talk

Open your calendar and make two entries in your schedule:
1. Block off two potential meeting times for a Heart Talk.
2. Write into your calendar the date and time this week when you will reach out to another person—or group—to invite them to participate in a Heart Talk with you.

Add to Your Life Success Journal

Turn to page 235 of *Your Life Success Journal* and complete the exercise for this chapter.

Success
and
Money

I have concluded that wealth is a state of mind, and that anyone can acquire a wealthy state of mind by thinking rich thoughts.

ANDREW YOUNG
American Politician, Diplomat, Pastor, and Activist

CHAPTER

17

DEVELOP A POSITIVE MONEY MIND-SET*

I've been rich, and I've been poor. Rich is better.

SOPHIE TUCKER
Singer, Comedian, Actor, and Radio Personality

Many people have a complicated relationship with money. Some people struggle their entire lives to earn just a little bit more. Others have lots of money, but still feel desperate about not having enough. You are probably aware that to have the success you want, you need to master the money game. This includes the practical *external* ways of generating more income, as well as ways of keeping spending in check. But it also includes handling the *internal* issues—the sometimes unconscious beliefs, thoughts, and feelings you may have about money that keep you stuck where you are.

IDENTIFY YOUR LIMITING BELIEFS ABOUT MONEY

When we are young and learning about the world, we also learn our beliefs about money from those closest to us. When you were growing up, did you hear phrases like these?

- *Money doesn't grow on trees.*
- *There's not enough money to go around.*
- *It's selfish to want a lot of money.*
- *You have to have money to make money.*
- *The rich get richer, and the poor get poorer.*
- *You have to work too hard to get money.*

---

*Read *Principle 56: Develop a Positive Money Consciousness* in the book *The Success Principles* for more explanation, stories, and examples.

- *Money is the root of all evil.*
- *People with money are evil, selfish, and unethical.*
- *Rich people are greedy and dishonest.*
- *You can't buy happiness.*
- *The more money you have, the more problems you have.*
- *If you're rich, you can't be spiritual.*

Some people take on even more negative beliefs about money as they grow up, and they never stop to challenge whether these beliefs are true. Do any of the following sound familiar to you?

- *Wealth brings pain and misery.*
- *It's not okay to make more money than my father/my mother, my brother, my sister.*
- *Becoming rich would violate some unspoken family code.*
- *If I become wealthy, people will resent me.*

THREE STEPS TO TURN AROUND YOUR LIMITING BELIEFS ABOUT MONEY

If you want to be more successful, you need to take charge of how you think about money and wealth. You can change any negative childhood programming by using a simple yet powerful three-step technique for replacing your limiting beliefs with more positive and empowering ones. You can do this exercise on your own, but it's even more powerful—and more fun—to do it with a partner or in a small group of people.

1. *Write down your limiting belief.*

   For our example, we will use this one: *Money is the root of all evil.*

2. *Challenge, make fun of, and argue with that limiting belief.*

   You do this by brainstorming a list of new beliefs that challenge the old ones. The more outrageous and fun you make them, the more powerful the resulting shift in your mind-set will be.

Here are several examples:

- *Money is the root of all philanthropy.*
- *Money is the root of all great vacations!*
- *Money may be the root of evil for someone who is evil, but I am a loving, generous, compassionate, and kind person who will always use money to create good in the world.*

You'll find it helpful to write out your new money beliefs on 3" × 5" index cards and add them to your affirmations to be read aloud with enthusiasm and passion every day. Making this part of your daily routine will go a long way toward helping you create what you want in the area of money and wealth.

3. Create a positive "turnaround statement."

Once you've taken the power out of the limiting belief with the step above, it's time to create a new statement that is the opposite of the original belief. You want this "turnaround statement" to send shivers of delight through your body when you say it. Once you have written it, walk around the room for a few moments repeating the new statement aloud. As you speak it, increase your energy and passion so that you feel it emotionally. Repeat this new belief several times a day for a minimum of 30 days, and it will be yours forever.

Here's an example of a turnaround statement:

When it comes to me, money is the root of love, joy, and good works.

Remember, these new ideas about your financial success will never form just by themselves! You have to keep repeating, thinking, and affirming these new thoughts to build your new beliefs about money and prosperity. Take time each day and focus on thoughts of abundance and prosperity, and images of financial success. As you continue to focus on these new thoughts and images, they will begin to crowd out and replace the old limiting beliefs and images. But here's the most important point: If you want to achieve your financial goals, you need to practice saying positive money affirmations (and visualizing the results you want) every single day.

Here are more positive money affirmations I have used with great success in my life:

I now have more money than I need to do everything I want to do.

All of my investments are profitable.

Money comes to me in many unforeseen and unexpected ways.

God is my infinite supply, and large sums of money come to me quickly and easily for the highest good of all concerned.

Every day, my income increases whether I am working, playing, or sleeping.

People love to pay me money for what I most love to do.

I am making positive choices about what to do with my money.

You can plant any idea into your subconscious mind by the repetition of thoughts *infused with positive expectancy*—and the intensely felt emotion associated with already having achieved what you want.

There is a science of getting rich, and it is an exact science, like algebra or arithmetic. There are certain laws that govern the process of acquiring riches, and once these laws are learned and obeyed by anyone, that person will get rich with mathematical certainty.

WALLACE D. WATTLES
Author of *The Science of Getting Rich*

DISCOVERING MORE ABOUT YOU
Identify Your Limiting Beliefs About Money

1. In the spaces below, list all of the limiting beliefs you have about money that you can think of. Use more space if you need it.

_____

_____

_____

_____

_____

_____

_____

_____

_____

_____

_____

_____

_____

_____

_____

_____

_____

_____

2. Circle or check mark (✓) the ones above that have the most power over you, or that you tend to continue to believe.

Three Steps to Turning Around Your Limiting Beliefs About Money

1. Review the list of items you circled in the exercise above. Select the one that is your number one limiting belief about money and write it here.

_____

_____

_____

_____

2. Now, challenge, make fun of, and argue with that limiting belief. Write your responses below.

_____

_____

_____

_____

_____

_____

_____

_____

_____

3. Create a positive turnaround statement and write it below.

_____

_____

_____

_____

DECIDE WHAT BEING WEALTHY MEANS TO YOU

Do you know how much wealth you want? Some people I know want to retire as millionaires, whereas others want to retire with $30 million or even $100 million. There is no right or wrong financial goal to have. But you do have to decide what *you* want.

When creating wealth in your life, remember that there is the life you want to live now and the life you want to live in the future. The life you are currently living is a result of the thoughts you have thought, the choices you made, and the actions you've taken in the past.

The life you live in the future will be the result of today's thoughts, choices, and actions. You need to determine and decide precisely how much money you'll need to live the lifestyle of your dreams. If you don't know, research how much it would cost you to do and buy everything you want throughout the next year. This could include rent or mortgage, food, clothes, medical care, automobiles, utilities, education, vacations, recreation, insurance, savings, investments, philanthropy, and anything else you want.

In the exercises that follow, you'll have the opportunity to create new beliefs about money and to refresh your vision for the wealth you desire.

DISCOVERING MORE ABOUT YOU:
What Does Being Wealthy Mean to You?

Think back to what you dreamed about and decided in *Chapter 3: Decide What You Want: Envision Your Ideal Life*. On page 43, you wrote your financial goals. Take a moment to look at those now. Using that information, or by creating new goals, complete the following sentences.

1. I will have a net worth of $_____ by the year _____.

2. I will earn at least $_____ by December 31st next year.

3. I will save and invest $_____ or _____% every month.

4. A new financial habit I will develop starting now is:

_____

_____

_____

_____

_____

_____

_____ .

5. I will be debt free by _____ / _____ / _____ .

6. To become debt free, I will:

_____

_____

_____

_____

_____

_____

_____ .

MAKE-IT-A-HABIT WORKSHEET
Your Money

1. This week, keep track of what you earn and what you spend each day. Make a note in your calendar to do this each day.

2. Make an appointment with yourself each month to record both your total income and your overall spending. Write this recurring event into your calendar for the end of each month.

3. Make an appointment with yourself for each quarter to determine your net worth. (If you are not sure how to do this, do a Google search for "How to determine personal net worth.") Write this recurring event into your calendar for the end of each quarter.

4. Each month, select one book to read, one Web site to follow, or one video to watch to become more financially literate.

Some recommended books, blogs, and podcasts to start with are:

• *40 Unbreakable Laws of Money* by Wayne Wakefield

• *The Richest Man in Babylon* by George S. Clason

• *The Wealthy Barber* by David Chilton

• *The Total Money Makeover* by Dave Ramsey

- *The Automatic Millionaire* by David Bach
- *The Millionaire Next Door* by Thomas J. Stanley and William D. Danko
- *The Billion Dollar Secret* by Rafael Badziag
- *Secrets of the Millionaire Mind* by T. Harv Eker
- *Rich Dad Poor Dad* by Robert T. Kiyosaki
- *Your Money or Your Life* by Vicki Robin
- *Money for the Rest of Us* (podcast) with David Stein
- *Stacking Benjamins* (podcast) with Joe Saul-Sehy
- FinancialSamurai.com (blog) with Sam Dogen

Add to Your Life Success Journal

Turn to page 236 of *Your Life Success Journal* and complete the exercise for this chapter.

YOUR LIFE SUCCESS JOURNAL

Answer the questions below to help you capture the most important insights you learned from all 17 chapters of this *Workbook*. Later, at any time, you can review what you have written here, and remind yourself of your progress.

CHAPTER 1: TAKE 100% RESPONSIBILITY FOR YOUR LIFE

Write down what you most want to remember in each of the four areas covered in this chapter, which started on page 3.

Blaming: _____

_____

Complaining: _____

_____

Making Excuses: _____

_____

E + R = O: _____

_____

CHAPTER 2: BE CLEAR WHY YOU'RE HERE: DETERMINE YOUR LIFE PURPOSE

"Discovering More About You" Guided Meditation

After listening to the guided meditation referred to on page 28, write a brief description or draw a picture of the gift you received during the meditation.

_____

_____

_____

_____

_____

_____

_____

_____

_____

_____

Life Purpose Statement

Write your life purpose statement here, from page 32.

_____

_____

_____

Chapter Conclusion

1. What was most valuable for you about this chapter?

_____

_____

_____

_____

_____

_____

Your Life Success Journal

2. What will it mean to you now that you have determined your life purpose?

_____

_____

_____

_____

_____

_____

_____

_____

_____

_____

CHAPTER 3: DECIDE WHAT YOU WANT: ENVISION YOUR IDEAL LIFE

Keep Your Vision Alive

Select the most important item from each of the seven areas of "wants" you wrote in *Chapter 3*, starting on page 43. Write each one below.

Finances _____

Work, Career, or Business _____

Relationships _____

Health and Fitness _____

Free Time, Fun, and Recreation _____

Personal and Spiritual Growth _____

Possessions _____

Making a Difference and Being of Service _____

CHAPTER 4: USE THE POWER OF GOAL-SETTING TO ACHIEVE YOUR VISION

Write down the three goals you wrote on page 69 to help you reach your vision.

Area of Your Vision	Goal (How Much, by When)
1.	
2.	
3.	

Want to keep going? Write five remaining goals (one in each area) that you'll need to work on in order to make progress in all eight areas of your vision. As a reminder, the eight areas are:

- Your Finances
- Your Work, Career, or Business
- Your Relationships
- Your Health and Fitness
- Your Free Time, Fun, and Recreation
- Your Personal and Spiritual Growth
- Your Possessions
- Making a Difference and Being of Service

Area of Your Vision	Goal (How Much, by When)
4.	
5.	
6.	
7.	
8.	

Write down your new, ambitious, Breakthrough Goal! Write it big and write it proudly!

_____

_____

Write a letter to yourself in the space below that will support you whenever you waver in your pursuit of these goals. Describe why reaching this goal is important to you. Describe what it will cost you if you don't achieve it.

Dear _____ (your name),

If you start to lose faith or find it overwhelming or scary to continue working toward the goals you set, remember this:

_____

_____

_____

_____

CHAPTER 5: USE AFFIRMATIONS AND VISUALIZATIONS

Affirmations and Visualizations

Take advantage of the power of repetition by writing your affirmations again be-low. When you list them here, it will also serve as an archive of your work in this *Workbook* and give you ready access later to what you have created today.

My Affirmation #1: _____

_____

_____

_____

My Affirmation #2: _____

_____

_____

_____

My Affirmation #3: _____

_____

_____

_____

My Affirmation for my Breakthrough Goal: _____

_____

_____

_____

Make a note on your calendar to revisit this page after you have repeated your affirmations for one week. When the date arrives, use the space below to write about your experience of using your affirmations. Do your affirmations seem more real to you now? What benefit do you see from repeating your affirma-tions?

_____

_____

_____

Make a note on your calendar to revisit this page one week after you have created your Vision Board. When the date arrives, use the space below to write about your experience of creating your Vision Board and viewing it multiple times each day. Does your vision seem more real to you now? What benefit do you see from spending time with your vision board each day?

_____

_____

_____

CHAPTER 6: BELIEVE IT'S POSSIBLE

List three major goals you have decided to believe you can achieve. I recommend you include your Breakthrough Goal as one of them.

1. _____

2. _____

3. _____

This week, tell your friends and family about what you now believe you can achieve. Check here when complete.

_____ Friends

_____ Family

When you have completed seven days of the Mirror Exercise, write down how it feels to acknowledge yourself day after day:

_____

_____

_____

_____

_____

CHAPTER 7: TAKE ACTION!

What advice will you give to yourself this week in order to stick with your plan for taking action according to the schedule you have set?

_____

_____

_____

To be human means that you might miss some of the scheduled dates for the action steps you set. If this happens, what will you say to yourself in order to forgive yourself and get yourself back on track?

_____

_____

_____

To reaffirm your desire to reach your Breakthrough Goal, write your affirmation for your Breakthrough Goal below, and then say it aloud.

_____

_____

_____

CHAPTER 8: EVERYTHING YOU WANT IS
ON THE OTHER SIDE OF FEAR

Your Evening Review

Every evening this week, take several minutes to further strengthen your resolve regarding fear. You can do this by conducting an Evening Review after dinner or before you go to bed. Here are the instructions for an Evening Review:

Close your eyes, take a few deep breaths, and say to yourself, "Show me where fear showed up in my life today." As you sit in silence, you will notice memories from the day beginning to emerge. For example, you may recall, *I was afraid to call that person who my friend said might be able to help me with my career decision. I hesitated because I was worried this new person would judge me as being indecisive about what I want.* Or, *I was going to sign up today for my first 10K run, but then I was afraid I might be wasting the $35 if I chicken out later.*

Once you have recalled the incidents of being afraid from earlier in the day, replay the situation in your mind, and this time see yourself taking the desired action and having the success you want, and allow yourself to experience whatever positive feelings may arise. Since your body can't tell the difference between a real event and an imagined event, you will be building your inner confidence to take more actions in the face of fear in the future.

CHAPTER 9: ASK WITHOUT FEAR OF REJECTION

You've made a lot of behavioral changes as you practiced asking without fear of rejection. In the space below, record the one thing you'll do differently as a result of reading this chapter.

_____

_____

_____

_____

_____

CHAPTER 10: ASK FOR FEEDBACK EARLY AND OFTEN

Use the following prompts to journal about the insights you're learning about feedback.

In what ways was asking for feedback easier than you expected?

_____

_____

What new lesson did you learn from your experience of asking for feedback?

_____

_____

Now it's time to give yourself some feedback—after all, you know yourself best. You especially know the areas where you have developed your strengths.

What three strengths of yours will most contribute to your future success?

Strength #1 _____

_____

Strength #2 _____

_____

Strength #3 _____

_____

What three areas of improvement will most contribute to your success?

Improvement area #1 _____

_____

Improvement area #2 _____

_____

Improvement area #3 _____

_____

CHAPTER 11: PRACTICE PERSISTENCE

Reinforce your commitment to persist now that you are in this strong state of mind. After all, persisting is up to you. Make a promise to yourself to continue working on your goal(s) in spite of any future obstacles. Refer back to this page if you ever start to think of quitting.

Example: *My positive intention to persist in spite of any future obstacles is:*

> *I realize that it is going to be a challenge to start my new coaching business. There will be times when I will worry about publishing new content on my Web site; I may hesitate when I need to pick up the phone and call a potential new client. But I will hang in there. I choose to be successful in this new venture, and no matter what happens, I will continue to persevere and find a way!*

My positive intention to persist in spite of any future obstacles is:

_____

_____

_____

_____

_____

_____

_____

_____

_____

_____

CHAPTER 12: PRACTICE MEDITATION

Once you have practiced meditating for one week, write in your journal about your experience.

What did you enjoy most about it?

_____

_____

_____

_____

_____

_____

_____

_____

What part, if any, was challenging for you?

_____

_____

Do you believe this would be a useful practice for you? Why or why not?

_____

_____

Is there a commitment that feels right to you about sustaining a meditation and mindfulness practice? If so, what is your commitment?

_____

Do you want to add that commitment to your calendar so that you will be reminded? If yes, add it now.

CHAPTER 13: CLEAN UP YOUR MESSES AND YOUR INCOMPLETES

At the end of this week, record the incompletions you have resolved. After each one, describe how it feels to make this progress.

Incomplete Resolved: _____

How do you feel about your progress? _____

_____

_____

Incomplete Resolved: _____

    How do you feel about your progress? _____

_____

_____

Incomplete Resolved: _____

    How do you feel about your progress? _____

_____

_____

Incomplete Resolved: _____

    How do you feel about your progress? _____

_____

_____

Incomplete Resolved: _____

    How do you feel about your progress? _____

_____

_____

CHAPTER 14: SURROUND YOURSELF WITH SUCCESSFUL PEOPLE

What I Learned from This Chapter

The most important things I learned from this chapter are: _____

_____.

How I intend to benefit from spending time with the people I identified in this chapter:

_____

_____

CHAPTER 15: START A MASTERMIND GROUP AND WORK WITH AN ACCOUNTABILITY PARTNER

Make a list of at least five people you will contact to see if they are willing to be your accountability partner.

1. _____

2. _____

3. _____

4. _____

5. _____

Call each person this week, and continue your calls to these or others until you have found an accountability partner. Once you have an accountability partner, journal below about the benefits you expect to achieve from this new productivity booster:

_____

_____

_____

_____

_____

_____

_____

_____

CHAPTER 16: HAVE A HEART TALK

Once you have conducted a Heart Talk this week, journal about your experience. Write about the value you received and what opened up for you—within yourself and within the relationship(s).

_____

_____

_____

_____

_____

_____

_____

_____

_____

_____

_____

_____

_____

_____

CHAPTER 17: DEVELOP A POSITIVE MONEY MIND-SET

What will you do this week to maintain a positive money mind-set about reaching your income goals for next year?

_____

_____

_____

Reflect on what having wealth would mean to you. How would it change your experience of your life?

_____

_____

_____

What are some practices you will use to shift your thinking about the amount of income you want to earn next year, and the amount of wealth you want to accumulate over the next 20 years?

_____

_____

_____

_____

Is there a promise you want to make to yourself about how you will think differently about money? If so, write it here.

_____

_____

_____

_____

SUGGESTED READING AND
ADDITIONAL RESOURCES FOR SUCCESS

*You are the same today as you'll be in five years except for two
things, the books you read and the people you meet.*

CHARLIE "TREMENDOUS" JONES
Member of the National Speakers Hall of Fame

I recommend that you read something educational, motivational, or inspirational every day—20 minutes a day minimum, an hour a day preferred. Below is a short list of some of my books to get you started. Get a list of the books I have found most useful on my success journey (almost 200 of them) at: JackCanfield.com/workbook-resources. There are enough books there to keep you busy for several years.

I suggest you read through the list on the Web site, see which books jump out at you, and start with those. Follow your interests and you'll find that each book you read will lead you to other books. There is also a list of audio programs I suggest you listen to, as well as videos and movies you might want to watch and several training programs conducted by others that I encourage you to attend. There are even two success-oriented summer camps I recommend for your kids.

We constantly update this list with the best new resources that I discover.

Here is a short list of my books that focus on success, as well as a few classics by others. They are all available at JackCanfield.com, Amazon.com, BarnesandNoble.com, and Books aMillion.com, as well as many of your local bookstores.

The Success Principles™: How to Get from Where You Are to Where You Want to Be (10th Anniversary Edition) by Jack Canfield and Janet Switzer. New York: William Morrow, 2015.

The Success Principles for Teens by Jack Canfield and Kent Healey. Deerfield Beach, FL: Health Communications, 2008.

How to Get from Where You Are to Where You Want to Be by Jack Canfield. London, UK: Harper Element, 2017.

The Aladdin Factor: How to Ask For and Get Anything You Want in Life by Jack Canfield and Mark Victor Hansen. New York: Berkley, 1995.

The Power of Focus Tenth Anniversary Edition: How to Hit Your Business, Personal and Financial Goals with Absolute Certainty by Jack Canfield, Mark Victor Hansen, and Les Hewitt. Deerfield Beach, FL: Health Communications, 2011.

Tapping into Ultimate Success: How to Overcome Any Obstacle and Skyrocket Your Results by Jack Canfield and Pamela Bruner. Carlsbad, CA: Hay House, 2012.

Jack Canfield's Key to Living the Law of Attraction: A Simple Guide to Creating the Life of Your Dreams by Jack Canfield and Dee Dee Watkins. Deerfield Beach, FL: Health Communications, 2007.

Success Affirmations: 52 Weeks for Living a Passionate and Purposeful Life by Jack Canfield with Ram Ganglani and Kelly Johnson. Deerfield Beach, FL: Health Communications, 2017.

The Power of Positive Inking: Color Your Way to Success (an adult coloring book with 35 principles of success) by Jack Canfield. Deerfield Beach, FL: Health Communications, 2017.

Coaching for Breakthrough Success: Proven Techniques for Making Impossible Dreams Possible by Jack Canfield and Peter Chee. New York: McGraw Hill, 2013. (This is a book for coaches and managers who want to coach people based on the success principles.)

The 30-Day Sobriety Solution: How to Quit or Cut Back Drinking in the Privacy of Your Own Home by Jack Canfield and Dave Andrews. New York: Atria Books, 2016.

The Original Chicken Soup for the Soul®: All Your Favorite Original Stories Plus 20 Bonus Stories (20th Anniversary Edition) by Jack Canfield, Mark Victor Hansen, and Amy Newmark. Cos Cob, CT: Chicken Soup for the Soul Publishers, 2013.

Chicken Soup for the Soul: Think Positive: 101 Inspirational Stories about Counting Your Blessings and Having a Positive Attitude by Jack Canfield, Mark Victor Hansen, and Amy Newmark. Cos Cob, CT: Chicken Soup for the Soul Publishers, 2010.

Think and Grow Rich by Napoleon Hill. The Napoleon Hill Foundation, 2016.

Think and Grow Rich: A Black Choice by Dennis P. Kimbro, Ph.D. New York: Ballantine, 1997.

The 7 Habits of Highly Effective People by Steven R. Covey. New York: Fireside, 1989.

Unlimited Power by Tony Robbins. New York: Simon & Schuster, 1986.

You Were Born Rich by Bob Proctor. Willowdale, ONT, Canada: McCrary Publishing, 1984.

The Seven Spiritual Laws of Success by Deepak Chopra. San Rafael, CA: Amber-Allen, 1994.

The Compound Effect by Darren Hardy. New York: Vanguard Press, 2012.

The One Thing: The Surprisingly Simple Truth Behind Extraordinary Results by Gary Keller. Austin, TX: Bard Press, 2013.

The Secret: 10th Anniversary Edition by Rhonda Byrne. New York: Atria/Beyond Words, 2006.

Homeless to Billionaire: The 18 Principles of Wealth Attraction and Creating Unlimited Opportunity by Andres Pira. Charleston, SC: Forbes Books, 2019.

The Billion Dollar Secret: 20 Principles of Billionaire Wealth and Success by Rafael Badziag. St Albans, Herts, UK: Panoma Press Ltd., 2019.

Audio Programs

The Success Principles: Your 30-Day Journey from Where You Are to Where You Want to Be by Jack Canfield and Janet Switzer is a 30-day audio home study course that is another great supplement to *The Success Principles*. Available at JackCanfield.com.

Self-Esteem and Peak Performance by Jack Canfield (Nightingale-Conant). Available at Amazon.com.

Maximum Confidence by Jack Canfield (Nightingale-Conant). Available at Amazon.com.

The Aladdin Factor by Jack Canfield and Mark Victor Hansen. Available at Amazon.com.

The Ultimate Jack Canfield Library (Nightingale-Conant). Available on Audible and at Amazon
.com.

Movies

Soul of Success: The Jack Canfield Story, produced by Nick Nanton, 2018. Available on Amazon
Prime.
The Secret, produced by Rhonda Byrne, et al. 2007. Available from Amazon.com.
The Secret Teachers Recorded Live. Audible Audiobook available on Amazon.com.
Teachers of The Secret—Jack Canfield. Available from Amazon.com.

Online Courses

Breakthrough to Success by Jack Canfield. This is the online version of my live five-day transformational training based on The Success Principles. Available at JackCanfield.com.
Your Extraordinary Life Program by Jack Canfield. Available at JackCanfield.com.
Train the Trainer Online. If you'd like to become a certified trainer of The Success Principles,
you can learn more about my online Train the Trainer Certification Program—now
with more than 1,000 certified trainers in 117 countries—at JackCanfield.com.
Bestseller Blueprint Online by Jack Canfield and Steve Harrison. An online course for authors
who want to make their books bestsellers. Available at BestsellerBlueprint.com.

Live Training Programs Based on The Success Principles

Breakthrough to Success is my flagship five-day or three-day training usually held in Scotts-
dale, Arizona, Southern California, or in other major cities in the United States.
One Day to Greatness is a one-day training held in various cities around the United States and
Canada. For a schedule, go to JackCanfield.com.
Train the Trainer (for The Success Principles) is our two-week live certification training to teach
The Success Principles and the Canfield Methodology. Usually limited to 50 serious
students. By application. More information at JackCanfield.com.
Luxury Executive Mastermind Retreat. This is a four-day intensive mastermind retreat limited
to 24 people usually conducted in a luxury resort hotel or villa in Santa Barbara, California, or in places like Maui, Dubai, Bali, or Florence, Italy. Information at JackCanfield
.com.

Coaching

If you'd like to work one-on-one over the telephone or online with a personal coach, you
can talk with one of our Canfield Coaches by calling 805-881-5191.

ABOUT THE AUTHORS

Jack Canfield, known as America's #1 Success Coach, is a bestselling author, professional speaker, trainer, and entrepreneur. He is the founder and chairman of The Canfield Training Group, which trains entrepreneurs, educators, corporate leaders, sales professionals, and motivated individuals in how to expand their vision and accelerate the achievement of their personal and professional goals.

As the creator of the beloved *Chicken Soup for the Soul*® series and the driving force behind the development and sales of more than 200 *Chicken Soup for the Soul*® books, with 100 million copies sold in the United States (and 500 million worldwide in 43 languages), Jack is uniquely qualified to talk about success. Jack's nationally syndicated newspaper column is read in 150 papers. The *Chicken Soup for the Soul*® television series aired on both the PAX and ABC networks.

Jack is a graduate of Harvard, holds a master's degree in psychological education from the University of Massachusetts, and has three honorary doctorates. Over the past 49 years, he has been a psychotherapist, an educational consultant, a corporate trainer, and a leading authority in the areas of self-esteem, breakthrough success, personal transformation, and peak performance.

The book *The Success Principles*™ has sold a million copies in 30 languages around the globe. Jack's other bestselling books—*The Success Principles for Teens, The Power of Focus, The Aladdin Factor, Dare to Win, You've Got to Read This Book!, The Key to Living the Law of Attraction, Coaching for Breakthrough Success*, and *Tapping into Ultimate Success*—have sold millions of copies and have launched complementary multimedia programs, coaching programs, and corporate training programs to enthusiastic individuals and corporations.

Jack holds a Guinness World Record title for having seven books on the *New York Times* bestsellers list on the same day (May 24, 1998). He also achieved a Guinness World Record title for the largest book signing (held for *Chicken Soup for the Kid's Soul*).

Jack is also the founder of The Foundation for Self-Esteem, which provides self-esteem resources and trainings to social workers, welfare recipients, and human resource professionals. Jack wrote and coproduced the GOALS Program, a video-based training program to help people in California transition from welfare to work, which has helped 810,000 people get off welfare.

Jack has appeared on more than 1,000 radio and television programs, including *Oprah, Oprah's SuperSoul Sunday, The Montel Williams Show, Larry King Live*, the *Today* show, *Fox & Friends*, the *CBS Evening News*, the *NBC Nightly News*, and CNN's *Talk Back Live*, and on PBS and the BBC. Jack is a featured teacher in 20 movies, including *The Secret, Soul of Success, The Truth, The Opus, Choice Point, The Tapping Solution*, and *The Keeper of the Keys*.

Jack has conducted more than 2,500 trainings, workshops, and seminars—and has presented and conducted workshops for more than 500 corporations, professional associations, universities, school systems, and mental health organizations in all 50 states and 51 countries. His clients include Microsoft, Federal Express, Siemens, Campbell's Soup Company, Virgin Records, Sony Pictures, General Electric, Sprint, Merrill Lynch, Hartford Insurance, Johnson & Johnson, Coldwell Banker, Northrop, RE/MAX, Keller Williams, UCLA, YPO, the U.S. Department of the Navy, and the Children's Miracle Network.

Jack has been inducted into the National Speakers Association Speakers Hall of Fame, is a recipient of the Rotary Club's Paul Harris Fellowship, was awarded the Golden Plate Award from the National Achievement Summit, and received the Chancellor's Medal from the University of Massachusetts. He was twice named Motivator of the Year by *Business Digest* magazine, received the Speaker of the Year Award from the Society of Leadership and Success, and is a recipient of the National Leadership Award and the Champion's Award from the National Association for Self-Esteem.

To find out more about Jack's Breakthrough to Success Trainings, Train the Trainer Program, Coaching Programs, and audio and video programs, or to inquire about hiring him as a keynote speaker, workshop facilitator, or trainer, you can contact his office at:

The Canfield Training Group, P.O. Box 30880, Santa Barbara, CA 93130
Phone: (805) 563-2935 and (800) 237-8336; fax: (805) 563-2945
E-mail: info@JackCanfield.com
Web site: JackCanfield.com

Brandon Hall, Ph.D., coaches individuals and teams on mission-driven high achievement and provides keynote talks to companies and conferences through his company, Next-Achievement.com. He has a doctorate in behavioral psychology and has been a student and a teacher of high performance for decades. His focus is on helping others identify what is most important to them and how they want to contribute to others, and supporting them with the most direct action plan to make that happen.

His doctoral research on best practices for time management and his master's research on weight control preceded his design of a training program on peak performance and another on the power of purpose. He wrote the first book, *Web-Based Training Cookbook*, about online learning for organizations, and provided the clarion call for the use of technology in business learning, beginning in 1994 with a newsletter, research reports, and many conference keynote talks, and developed a global reputation.

He has written for *Forbes* magazine twice, and for 10 years was a columnist for *Chief Learning Officer* magazine.

Brandon has advised many organizations, including IBM, Apple, GE, Kraft, Cisco, Exxon, 3M, Microsoft, the Department of Defense, and many others. He has been interviewed by the *New York Times,* the *Wall Street Journal, Fortune, Business Week, Inc., Fast Company, Training, T&D, HR Executive,* and others. He has been a featured speaker at conferences around the world including North America, Europe, Asia, Australia, and the Middle East. He has taught classes at San Francisco State University and has been an invited speaker at Harvard University and Stanford University.

To find out more about Brandon's coaching and speaking services, visit Next-Achievement .com, email info@next-achievement.com, or phone: 415-854-2043.

Janet Switzer has been at the forefront of helping celebrity authors, emerging thought leaders, and niche-market entrepreneurs expand their impact and grow their businesses for more than 30 years.

Her high-profile clients have included Jack Canfield, originator of the *Chicken Soup for the Soul*® book series; social-media personalities Dave Braun and Troy Amdahl, authors of *Oola: Find Balance in an Unbalanced World;* Lisa Nichols, author of *Abundance Now;* motivational speaker Les Brown; underground business guru Jay Abraham; and tapping-therapy founder Dr. Roger Callahan; among many other recognized authors and experts.

Today, Janet is the coauthor of the classic success book *The Success Principles*™, named by Noop Research as the #1 Book for Managers, Leaders, and Humans—now in 40 languages—as well as coauthor of the popular *The Success Principles*™ audio training program. In addition, she's the #1 bestselling author of *Instant Income: Strategies That Bring in the Cash for Small Businesses, Innovative Employees and Occasional Entrepreneurs*, from McGraw-Hill Publishers.

Janet has advised authors and small businesses—spanning dozens of diverse industries—in leveraging their expertise, intellectual assets, products, services, distribution channels, Internet presence, and other intangibles for countless millions in revenue. She is one of America's most respected authorities in the publishing and training industries, helping niche-market experts attain worldwide status and million-dollar incomes by building publishing empires around their training concepts, industry knowledge, or unique market posture. Since 1989, her consulting firm has advised 24 *New York Times* bestselling authors—contributing strategy, marketing campaigns, and content development to more than 75 *New York Times* bestselling books and associated learning tools.

Her books, newsletters, and training courses are read and used by authors and businesspeople in more than 80 countries, and she has traveled to nearly every continent speaking to thousands of entrepreneurs, independent sales professionals, corporate employees, and industry association members on the principles of success and income generation.

She has been a widely published journalist, began her professional career as a campaign specialist for a Member of the United States Congress, and is a former columnist with Nightingale-Conant's *AdvantEdge* magazine and *Training Magazine* (Asia Edition).

A popular media personality seen by more than 75 million viewers, she has been featured in the *Wall Street Journal, USA Today*, the *New York Times, Time Magazine, US Weekly, Entrepreneur Magazine, Publisher's Weekly, Costco Connection, MSNBC, Hour of Power from the Crystal Cathedral,* and countless other publications and radio and television shows.

Janet's specialized agency consults directly with authors and entrepreneurs who are ready to establish new income-generation systems in their businesses.

During her free time, Miss Switzer is an award-winning floral designer, design lecturer, and national flower show judge. She is a three-time winner of the prestigious Flower Arranger of the Year award for California, competes in flower shows throughout the western United States, and travels the world studying with top design instructors. Her modern, avant-garde designs have been featured in flower-arranging publications throughout the United States.

Miss Switzer lives in the greater Nashville, Tennessee, area. Please visit JanetSwitzer .com for more details and free resources for authors and small businesses.

SUCCESS PRINCIPLE #45:
Hire a Personal Coach

People who have coaches always achieve more than those who don't. Whether you call it mentoring, training, or Coaching, having some kind of one-on-one voaching program can help you accelerate your success.

Jack has trained and mentored a team of top-notch Coaches to provide you the personal support, objectivity, and constructive feedback you need to achieve success—in business and in life.

Go to CanfieldCoaching.com and receive a **FREE Personal Momentum Session** today and discover how Canfield Coaching can get you from where you are—to where you want to be.

Working with a Canfield Coach will:

- Help you clarify your vision and goals
- Support you through your fears
- Keep you focused on your highest priorities
- Confront your unconscious behaviors and old patterns
- Expect you to do your best – and hold you to it!
- Help you live by your values
- Show you how to earn more while working less
- Align with your core genius - and so much more with our customized programs

Request your complimentary momentum session with a Canfield coach today!

CanfieldCoaching.com

GET CERTIFIED AS A JACK CANFIELD SUCCESS PRINCIPLES TRAINER!

Join Our Team of Certified Trainers and Transform Your Life & Career

Become one of Jack Canfield's Certified Success Principles Trainers and learn the life-changing strategies he's developed over the past 40 years.

Train the Trainer is a professional development program where Jack personally instructs you how to teach his core Success Principles curriculum using the "Jack Canfield Methodology" of experiential learning and the holistic model of growth and development.

Whether you choose to study online in the convenience of your home or office, or attend the live training, you'll be equipped with the skill set, content, exercises, seminar design, and training tools to get results!

RECOMMENDED FOR:
- Trainers, speakers, coaches, and consultants
- Business leaders, managers, and human resources professionals
- Educators, professors, and administrators
- Therapists, psychologists, and counselors
- or ANYONE who wants to facilitate change, growth, and leadership in others

Learn More at: JackCanfield.com/trainings
or call 805-881-5191

MORE INSPIRING TITLES FROM
JACK CANFIELD

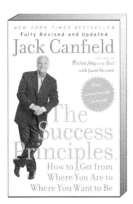

The Success Principles™ — 10th Anniversary Edition
How to Get from Where You Are to Where You Want to Be

In celebration of its 10th anniversary, this new edition of Jack Canfield's classic bestseller includes a brand new foreword and an afterword for succeeding in the digital age.

Jack Canfield's practical and inspiring guide has helped thousands of people transform themselves for success. Now, he has revised and updated his essential guidebook to reflect our changing times.

Taken together and practiced every day, these principles will change your life beyond your wildest dreams.

The Success Principles Workbook
An Action Plan for Getting from Where You Are to Where You Want to Be

This essential companion to the million-copy bestseller *The Success Principles* provides readers with a practical, step-by-step workbook to transform their lives.

Step-by-step instructions, incorporating self-discovery exercises, "Make It a Habit" worksheets, and journaling help keep readers on a path to success.

Whether you want to fulfill your professional and personal goals, boost your confidence, solve everyday obstacles, or work to achieve your deepest purpose, this indispensable book will provide the clarity you've been seeking to give you the future you've always wanted.

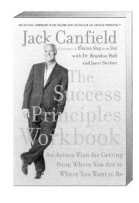

You've GOT to Read This Book!
55 People Tell the Story of the Book That Changed Their Life

This book puts the power of transformational reading into your hands. Jack Canfield, co-creator of the bestselling *Chicken Soup for the Soul*® series, and self-actualization pioneer Gay Hendricks have invited notable people to share personal stories of books that changed their lives. What book shaped their outlook and habits? Helped them navigate rough seas? Spurred them to satisfaction and success?

If you're looking for insight and illumination—or simply for that next great book to read—*You've Got to Read This Book!* has treasures in store for you.

HarperCollins*Publishers*